Never Stop!

Asking, discovering, and sharing!

Herbert I. Burns Jr.

For information contact :Herbert I Burns
Https://hibssb.myportfolio.com
Email: HerbBurns@mail.com

Book and Cover design by :Herbert I Burns Jr
Edited by: Susan Burns
ISBN: 978-1-09832-163-5

First Edition: December 2019

CONTENTS

Introduction

Have you ever been **asked** to stop doing something? In this book I **ask** you to Never Stop! That's right! Never stop asking, discovering, and sharing. You will be provided a pathway and procedures to **discover** what you never knew about your family, about working, and about your faith.

Don't wait until it's too late! I wish that I had access to a book like this years ago. You will be shown what to **ask**, and how to discover many things. You will learn from the stories of many others that through the act of **asking**, **discovering**, and **sharing**, there has been transformation in their lives and in the lives of others.

You can learn how to be a more effective transformer in someone's life with step by step directions for your family, your work, and your faith. Don't stop! No, no, never stop! Begin now with this book, and find new discoveries in, and for your life. You will be encouraged as you help others to **Never stop asking, discovering, and sharing.**

Don't stop here. Continue reading!

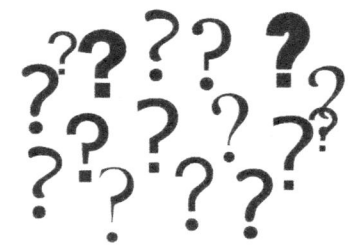

CHAPTER ONE

Why?

Never stop asking, discovering, and sharing! These three words have had profound meaning in my life, and in the lives of all of us. "Ask, discover, and share." These three words have resulted in new directions, new relationships, and have brought happiness to others. These three words have also revealed truths that have also caused pain and sufferings to others. Much like the foundation of a building these words become the materials and structures in our lives that can impact the lives of others through sharing about what we have asked and discovered.

This book is entirely different than my first book "Route 66 - Have You Found Your Route in Life", which is an illustrated journey through the Bible with scripture, history, and real-world applications. In this book I hope to encourage you to Never Stop! Asking, Discovering, and Sharing. We are not robots trained to do one repetitive task until that process has ended. God has created us all with a divine purpose, and He has given us all unique talents for asking and discovering (the internal), but it is through the sharing (the external), that we begin to fulfill His purpose for us. As we change, this purpose can and will affect the lives of others.

As you continue this journey "Never Stop!", I will share personal experiences about myself and share what others have experienced in their lives, as well. This journey will explore three areas of asking, discovering, and sharing.

In Chapter Two, we will explore the area of the family. I will share aspects of my life as a child, as a parent, and as a relative. I'll also share the consequences of asking, discovering and sharing. In Chapter Three, I will share about my work as a student, employee, educator, manager, administrator, and CEO. In Chapter Four, I will share information about faith as a questioner and as a believer. The fifth chapter will include testimonies of others sharing their life experiences regarding the words asking, discovering, and sharing. It is my hope that as you read this book, it will encourage you to Never Stop Asking, Discovering, and Sharing. And in the sixth and final chapter, the total pathway will be woven together for you to apply in your life.

Let's start with an understanding of the "**Ask**". This simple word is the beginning, and it is the spark that can kindle a flame or passion which might be just a flicker, and that could be here for the moment and then gone! Or it could evolve into a growing flame that can affect the lives of many peoples, economies, and nations. Just the way the word "ask" is framed, it can begin to establish direction for action. Here are a few examples:

Do you understand what I just asked you?

Can I ask you?

What did he ask you?

What did she ask you?

You were asked to do what?

What can you lose by asking?

You will never know unless you ask.

Have you ever heard any of those statements? When we ask, it could mean that we are beginning to gather data, perhaps inquiring for permission, looking for direction, or an invitation. I am reminded of:

Matthew 7 v7, "Ask, and it shall be given you; seek, and ye shall find; knock, and it shall be opened unto you."

So, for me it all starts with the knock or the first asking. For me, my favorite is, "What can you lose by asking?" I cannot begin to remember how many friends and colleagues that I have said this to as an encouragement for them to begin to act regarding something in which they have a vision or passion. If I am in the position to help them with their "ask", I will do all that I can to help fulfill their "ask."

My wife teases me occasionally when she asks me a question. My response many times is that I ask her something as my response. She says, "When I ask you something, you always question what I am asking." I guess that is because of the environment I was raised in, and mostly because of my architectural education, which I will talk about later. But remember:

Colossians 3 v23 "Whatever you do, work at it with all your heart, as working for the Lord, not for men."

Never, never, never be afraid to ask. Once the act of asking has taken place, next could be the discovery. This process of discovery could be extremely rewarding and wonderful and bring joy, or discovery could be something that you were hoping not to discover and could bring grief. Sometimes when the "ask" takes place, we might have a feeling in which direction the discovery might go, and in other cases we will not know until after the discovery. Be sure you have the necessary tools available to help you in the process, which I will talk about later. A variable noun word form of "discovery" is:

If someone makes a discovery, they become aware of something that they did not know before.

As you continue reading, I am sure that many things are coming to your mind that you have discovered in life, or have seen what others have discovered. A couple of scriptures come to mind regarding discovery.

Proverbs 3 v13 "Happy is the man who makes discovery of wisdom, and he who gets knowledge."

Matthew 7 v4 "For narrow is the door and hard the road to life. and only a small number make discovery of it."

I used to tell my students, "Reading is the key to the treasure chest of knowledge, and knowledge is your pathway to the future." Let's take a moment and look at some of the tools for discovery. The most important tool is you! You are the master tool that will allow you to craft the decisions and directions you take in life. Take a moment and reflect about yourself. Look at your talents, your strengths, and your weaknesses. These are the tools you take with you wherever you go. As for me, I believe that the greatest talent given to me can best be explained with the following statement:

"God has given me passion and vision. These are the fuels that drive me. With passion there is the love for what I do and a willingness to help others. Vision is the wind in my sails and releases the anchor to allow me to go where I have not yet been. Passion and vision strengthen me to enlighten, educate, enrich, engage, and empower others to do their best."
H.I.Burns

Once you have identified your talents for discovery, it becomes simpler to make the selections of all the other elements required to help you in the discovery process: mechanical tools, electronic tools, data, other people, etc. When you have assembled the appropriate tools, you can then begin to build and ignite the discovery engine. It is then up to you as to how hard you drive that engine of discovery and how well you take care of it during the discovery process. Some will blow the engine up, and others will see it through to the finish line of discovery.

As we begin to explore that wonderful and intriguing realm of discovery, minds and eyes are opened to what was once unknown. What exactly does discovery really mean? I did a web search with the word discovery, and what a discovery that was!

Discovery channel online

Discovery channel live

Discovery education

Discovery science

Discovery Clothing

Discovery -Wikipedia

Discovery-YouTube

Discovery Institute

These are just a few, and I could go on and on. It's really amazing what a web search can turn up these days. I can still remember the days before computer technology and how time consuming it was to collect data and specific information involving a discovery process. Now that there is an emerging digital explosion of knowledge, the pathway for finding information is becoming easier and easier, depending on the types of questions being **asked.**

When you think about discovery, what do you really think about? I would like you to take about ten seconds and write down what first comes to mind regarding discoveries.

Could it be:

Electricity

Penicillin

Atomic Bomb

Automobile

Space exploration

Cell phone

Computer

These discoveries are what first came to my mind, and they all seem to be tangible and physical. What about the intangible? These can also be a part of the ingredients of discovery. These intangibles are things that we are unable to touch or grasp. They do not have physical presence. They may not be able to be seen but still can cause affect and effect. We must never forget the power of intangible discoveries because in many cases it is these that become the foundations of strong and sustaining discoveries that can eventually impact the lives of many people.

So, I repeated the previous exercise, and let me ask you to do the same. Take ten seconds and write down some intangibles that might lead you to discoveries. Here is what came to me:

Love

Pain

Hope

Sharing

Faith

Prayer

Certainly, I know people who have discovered love, or love has discovered them, myself included. For me, love is the greatest motivator in my life for discovery. Without love I would have no energy to discover. I will discuss this more in coming chapters.

I am sure we all have at some point discovered pain in our life, perhaps physical and emotional, as well. Pain in my life has certainly led me to discover that change must take place if I don't want to go through that same type of pain again. It could be painful just to ask something, it could be painful to discover something, and yes, it can certainly be painful to share something.

For me, hope is vital in my discovery process. It is the hope that whatever discoveries I have encountered, that they will be of benefit to others. Also, that my discoveries might cause positive change in processes that can affect the lives of others. As you continue to read further, I hope that you will see how asking and discovering have influenced my life, your life, and in the lives of others.

Let's look at the third area, and probably the most important; **sharing**. What does sharing really mean to you? Is it a part of your job description? Can you recall when others have shared with you? Have you shared your heart with someone, your time, your money, your knowledge, or your faith? The Bible has some important words about sharing:

> *Proverbs 19 v17 "Whoever is kind to the poor lends to the LORD, and he will reward them for what they have done."*

> *Proverbs 22 v9 "The generous will themselves be blessed, for they share their food with the poor."*

> *Philippians 2 v3,4 "Do nothing out of selfish ambition or vain conceit. Rather, in humility value others above yourselves, not looking to your own interests but each of you to the interests of others."*

> *Proverbs 11 v24 "One person gives freely, yet gains even more, another withholds unduly, but comes to poverty. A generous person will prosper, whoever refreshes others will be refreshed."*

Sharing is your fuel to energize others. Sharing is your pathway to spread the word about knowing what you have discovered because you asked!

Faith is also something that I must not forsake. Faith is my complete trust or confidence in what I am doing, but that must also be coupled with another intangible, that of prayer. Prayer takes my faith, and it then becomes a conduit for me to share with my God and Savior, Jesus Christ, and to ask for direction and guidance in all that I might seek to do. Do not misunderstand what I am saying. There can still be failure along the way, but that is part of the pathway of discovery. Without these two coupled together, faith and prayer, sharing is like a car without wheels. It's not going to move in any direction.

We are coming full circle, back to the beginning premises of "Never Stop - Asking, Discovering, and Sharing." We have begun to explore the elements and relationships of those three words that can create change in our life and in the lives of others.

With my involvement in education and business for many years, sometimes words are not enough to explain my thoughts. There are times that a diagram or chart has needed to be created to help explain the process. If I had to make a diagram of the process of "Asking, Discovering, and Sharing", it would look something like this. See Figure 1 on the next page:

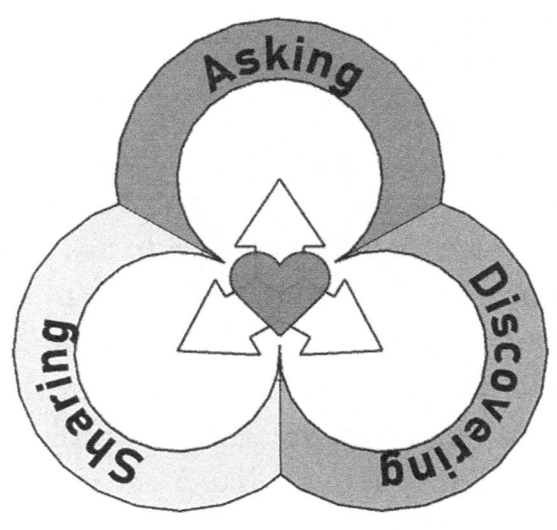

Figure 1

The important thing to remember is that everything must come from the heart. If your heart is not in whatever you are doing, ask yourself, "Why am I doing this?" Also, this process is bi-directional. Your ignitor can be anyone of these three (ask, discover, share), and the flow can be in any direction, as this is an organic dynamic process. You might ask, "What leads to discovery?" Then you share with others. You might be shown a discovery that leads you to ask questions. Someone might share something with you that leads you to ask questions which could result in a discovery. This now becomes the "Why" from which the first chapter of this book drew its title.

As you continue to read, it is my hope that you will discover and share life changing stories with your family and friends about what you have discovered from them, and you will create positive changes in their lives. As you continue your journey, I hope that you are blessed by the inspiration of others from their life experiences. When you are involved in asking, discovering, and sharing, you begin a new journey in your life. Let that journey now begin for you!

In the technological world we live in today, it is more important than ever to put down the phones, the tablets, etc., and to truly share with, and listen to stories as they are shared within the family unit. This will then ignite change and growth!

CHAPTER TWO

Family

Let's start by trying to understand what a family is. If you look on the internet at Wikipedia for a definition of "family", there is more information there than you could ever imagine explaining the meaning of family. There is the conjugal (nuclear) family, single parent family, matrifocal family, extended family, family of choice, blended family, and on and on. There are 170 citations of reference to family that cover everything from health, the law, abuse, legal marriage, etc., defining "family".

As I now look back, the word family was a simple idea for me, defined by my relationship with my parents and my relatives; those that have a biological connection with one another. Then along my life path, there have been those who showed me love, helped to lead me and to nurture me, and because of their help I have considered them family.

As I have matured, there are those outside of my biological family that I tried to treat like family; perhaps an employee, colleague, student, or friend. I don't know if they have considered me as family, but that's not what is important. What is important is that I have tried to provide them with the same love, help, and direction that I would want to extend to my own biological family. As you continue to read about family, I hope it will lead you to a time of asking, discovering, and sharing for yourself, not only to discover things about your family, but also to share with others the trials, tribulations, successes, and failures in your life. These stories might lead to a positive change within your family life or in other relationships.

Here is some of my personal story about family. It's January 15, 2019; 8:30AM, and I am home alone looking out my window in my home office at the forest. My wife has gone bowling with ladies from our Bible Fellowship class. It is our third day without electricity because of an ice storm. We are discovering how to live in a large home with only a gas fireplace to heat the house. I did not sleep well last night, as the only heat in our house is from the gas logs on the living floor. I am thinking about what I want to share about family as I begin this chapter. I will type until the battery is so low on my laptop computer that I have to stop.

Let me start with a flash back to my earliest memories about family so I can begin my sharing and discoveries with you. As you read, I would hope that you also might begin your journey with me as your recall what family life was like for you from childhood to adulthood and document it somehow so that it might be shared with your children, their children, and their children.

When I try to discover my memories from those early beginnings, they are vague, at most. I must have been 2 or 3 years old. We lived in a stone house on Lincoln Avenue in Lexington, Kentucky.

House on Lincoln Avenue

The living room opened into the dining room. There were stairs that led to a second-floor area, and I think there was a bedroom to the right of the stairs. I do remember a Christmas tree one year, and under the tree was my first train set. It was already set up, and the train went around the tree, but strangely, I don't remember much about my parents at all during this time, which I will come back to later. I can still close my eyes and recall playing in our neighbor's house across the street in a basement with a large open space. Our neighbor, as I remember, had a young son and daughter about my age, and we would run and chase each other while we were playing. We would ride tricycles around in that large open space. The room was dimly lit, as most basements were at that time. I still remember the sink and washing machine up against the masonry block wall, and sometimes there would be laundry hanging from a stretched-out rope, drying, as we would run and wander underneath them, pretending that they were something like a cloud canopy above us.

I am an only child. It wasn't until later in my young life that I **discovered** that my mom and dad wanted more children, and that my mother had three miscarriages, possibly. I was the incubator baby that made it. So, I could have had four siblings. I was told later that Mom had lost a set of twins and two other children. Then there is this large memory gap in my earliest childhood years. I don't know if I blocked things from my memory, or if I was a part of some secret experiment that erased my memory. Just Kidding! For whatever reason, my next family memories began with my aunt and uncle when I was in the 1st grade at Bryan Station School. Aunt Lillian was my mom's sister, and Duke Sr. was Lillian's husband. They had five children; Sphar and Nancy, the oldest two, were already out of the home and married. Then there was Ray, Becky, and Duke Jr. Duke was my age.

When I would **ask**, "Where are Mom and Dad?", I was told that Dad was out of town and that Anna, my mother, needed to be with him and would be back on the weekends. I don't remember crying or throwing temper tantrums. I may have!? But at that time, I was surrounded by a loving family; my aunt and uncle, and great cousins who became my accepted brothers and sister. They accepted me as a cousin/ brother.

My Uncle Duke's house was "out in the country", as we would say in Kentucky. Their house was on several acres, and there were chickens, roosters, a goat, a large vegetable garden about ½ acre in size, or so it seemed to me, and a concord grape arbor. There were apple and plum trees, and possibly another type of fruit tree. Not far from us were large horse farms, and beside us was a horse veterinarian. He had a large barn with several stalls for the horses. Duke and I would peek into the barn when no one was around. Behind my Uncle Duke's property was Mr. Lewis's property and barn. He raised tobacco, and every year we could watch the tobacco being cut and hung in the barn to dry. Later, Mr. Lewis became the assistant principal at Bryan Station High School where we attended, and our paths crossed again, but in a different way, which you will read about later.

There were always things going on at the house. Duke and I slept in bunk beds on the first floor, cousin Ray was in a bedroom next to us, and his sister Becky had a bedroom upstairs across from her parents. Duke and I had chores to do from time to time. We had to fetch eggs from the hen house. We had to stay far away from the rooster because he would chase us, and we didn't want to get spiked from the spurs on his feet. Oh, I forgot to mention that we had geese, also!

Another thing Duke and I were able to do, which I didn't really call a chore, was to remove the clinkers from the furnace. I need to stop writing now because my computer is getting ready to shut down due to a low battery! I will continue writing when we finally get power back to our house. Power is now back on after day three of the outage!

Clinker

Now back to those clinkers. Well, at my aunt and uncle's house, down in the furnace room, there was this gigantic gravity air-fed coal burning furnace. That means there were no fans to circulate the heat through the house so the heat would just rise and flow into each room naturally. That coal burning furnace looked like some kind of beast to us, with many gigantic arms coming out in every direction and extending to the floor above. There was a coal chute where we could send coal to the basement from the outside. My uncle had a self-feeding coal auger that would supply a steady stream of coal to the furnace. After a couple days of running the furnace, Duke and I would go down and pull the red-hot clinkers from the furnace. In case you did not know, clinkers are the burnt coal ash chunks. We would take long metal tongs, remove the clinkers, and put them in a coal bucket, which we would take out to the back yard. Then we would dump them beside the coal pile. Sometimes they would be hot and glowing. Each one was an amazing creation. That is one of the **asks** that we enjoyed, because of the amazing coal ash creations that were made, and that we were able to see!

What a great time it was in the winter for our families to **share** and **discover**! My aunt's and uncle's house always became a gathering place for family and friends. If it had snowed, we kids would be outside until darkness fell. Down the road, about half a mile away, was Faulkner Road. On that road was a long incline which was great for sled runs. Each of us spent serious time listening to my cousin Ray explain to us how to wax the runners on our sleds. He would then give us a wax candle so that we might prepare the runners on our own sled to make sure it was faster than the others. Everyone had a sled. Of course, we all built snow men, except for cousin Ray. I can still close my eyes and remember that one snow sculpture he made. One morning when we went out in the front yard, there it was! A beautiful, curvaceous, large-bosomed, long-haired snow woman! It was certainly a car stopper! Being the art major that he was, I think it represented his current girlfriend.

When we finally returned to the house after a day in the snow, we were greeted by a huge roaring fire in a fireplace, which seemed to take over a whole wall in the living room. For us, the fireplace seemed massive! It was about 4 ½ to 5 feet wide. As a young boy, I recall that their living room was extremely interesting, sort of like a military museum. Above the fireplace, and on the adjacent two walls hung civil war pistols, swords of all kinds; civil war swords, military dress swords, and swords belonging to fraternal organizations. There were long rifles, musket loaders, a Kentucky rifle, military rifles, and a Stiger WW1 rifle. I never found out where they came from, but they certainly stirred the imagination!

Then there was that winter moment I will never forget when I **asked** someone to do something that became physically and emotionally painful for them. Keep in mind that this happened before the 1983 movie, "Christmas Story". Yes, it was a cold and snowy day. We were outside playing, and yes, there was a metal framed swing set. You probably know what happened next! It was one of those **ask's** that causes pain to someone. Yes, I did cause pain. There was frost on the metal poles, and I asked my cousin Duke to take a lick and to tell me what the frost tasted like. I knew all the time what would happen. Well, happen, it did! Duke took a big lick on that pole, and his tongue instantly flash froze to the metal. It was stuck quite firmly. I tried breathing hot air on the metal, but that did not release his tongue. Finally, Duke pulled away, hollering! There on the metal pole was a part of his tongue! His tongue was bleeding, and he darted inside the house! I was not in a hurry to go inside at all, for I knew I was in deep trouble. When I finally inched my way into the house, Aunt Lillian was tending to Duke, and she read me the riot act! If I had been her biological son, I am certain that a spanking would have been delivered that day. Instead, she said that she was going to call my mother and tell her about the terrible thing I had done to her son. I knew consequences would be forthcoming. But the reason I was staying at Aunt Lillian's is because Mom was with Dad, so I was told, and it was many days before I was reprimanded. Time passed by, and things cooled off regarding my transgression. Duke and I made up and continued to act as brothers.

My Aunt Lillian with her children/my cousins from left to right-Lillian, Harold, Duke, Ray, Nancy, Sphar, and Becky.

In the above picture you see Harold, (foster child), who later joined the family when I was in high school and became another great cousin. My Uncle Duke is not pictured as he is the one who took this picture.

Living with my cousins during three of my formative years, was really a great experience! We laughed together, played together, and stuck together. Sometimes I felt like I was a guest, but mainly I was family. My cousin Ray had started at the University of Kentucky as an art major and had become one of the first male cheerleaders there. Becky was still in junior high school, being several years younger than Ray. Becky was the only girl in the house, and looking back on it now, it must have been challenging for her to have two brothers and a male cousin, all demanding time from her parents. Later in this story, my interactions with Becky grew, and I really felt like she was my sister, and I still feel that way today.

We took the bus to school every morning and at the end of the school day. As I shared before, Duke and I went to Bryan Station. At that time, it was 1st through 12th grades.

When you think back on your life, what do you remember from those first three years of school? I ask you to take time and write them down so that you might revisit your early discoveries to share with others later. Here are some things to think about:

What did the room look like?

Do you remember any of your teachers?

Can you describe the playground?

Where did you eat lunch?

Did you have to take naps?

Do you remember any of your class projects?

In those early years we would spend more waking hours at school than at home. You may remember more than I have about those times. I recall that in the first grade our class made a little red caboose. I believe it was to be a part of a school play. It was about as tall as a first grader with their hands held up straight. The skeletal frame was made from lathing strips that we taped together. We then skinned it with paper, painted it red, then painted windows on the side. That is the first school project I can ever remember. I don't remember seeing the play it was supposed to be in. The other thing I remember from first grade is the lunchroom. I can still visualize the long hall we walked down. Then we went down some very wide steps to a landing, then down another series of steps to the lower level, then down a short hallway to the cafeteria. Wow! For a first grader it was the largest room we got to go in. Aunt Lillian made our lunches at home, and we took them to school. After lunch, it was back up the stairs, and then it was nap time. Everyone had a nap cloth and a pillow. It was then a quiet time for all. It was probably the best time of the day for the teachers!

Well, as for the second grade, it is a total blank except that our classroom was across the hall from my first grade classroom.

There are some memories, and I guess you could say, battle scars, that remain with me today from my third grade experience. First, I will share the one good memory from third grade! We were studying geography, specifically, volcanos. I took my schoolbook home and was sharing some of the pictures with family, my cousins being my nuclear family. Ray said, "Let me show you how to make a volcano." He had some clay at the house, I guess from his art projects at the University, so we built a small clay volcano and carved out a small hole down the center. We filled the hole with baking powder, then added a few drops of vinegar, and wow! The volcano was foaming and running over the edge like a lava flow. **What a discovery** that was for me! I took the volcano to class. I remember all my classmates crowding around, watching the eruption. So, the act of **my sharing** the volcano pictures in my schoolbook with my cousin, led him to **ask** if I would like to build a volcano. Then **I discovered** how to do it! Another thing I remember from my third grade year was what cousin Ray did for us one day   He took three bars of soap and carved Duke, Becky, and me little boats. They were so cool! When we took baths, we floated those little soap boats in the tub. I still have childhood physical scars which came from another experience that I remember from third grade. We were in the school library at the time, which was about the size of a classroom, with shelves of books all around the walls. In the center of the library were tables where we could sit, read, or work on projects. Both wounds I received were at the hands of my female classmates. Battle One involved a shared eraser. The girl sitting next me had been using it, and I asked for the eraser. She said "No." I guess I looked at her with a mean little boy look and said, "Give me that eraser", with my hand outstretched. She replied by stabbing me with the pencil point in my outstretched open hand. The pencil lead broke off in my hand, and I still have that reminder 63 years later, with the lead stain still there under my skin. Well, I guess I didn't learn my lesson.

Battle Two took place that same year in the library. Again, I was pencil stabbed in the knee by another girl because I tried to grab some paper from her. I still have the mark on my knee from that lovely little girl! Isn't it amazing what we remember from our early years in grade school?

Those three years living with my cousins were truly amazing, and the experience would help guide me on my career path later in life. I was surrounded by family that loved me and cared for me. My Uncle Duke was a mail carrier during the day and would usually get to the house from work around 3:00. My Aunt Lillian worked the night shift as a nurse at the Shriners Hospital in Lexington, Ky. She would usually leave after we were in bed. So, my main memories are the times I had with my cousins and times at school in those early years.

During the days, whenever the weather permitted, we were told to go out and play, which we took as "Stay out of the house and play unless you need to go to the bathroom." We would play until we were tired, or until it started getting dark. We had to entertain ourselves, as there were no cell phones, no video games, and no computers at that time. We had a gigantic black walnut tree in the back yard. Hundreds of walnuts would fall on the ground in autumn. We would take a hammer and knock the husks off the shells. Our hands would be walnut stained for several weeks. We fed the chickens, played in the root cellar, played on the swings, laid in the hammock, played a lot of Indian ball, and played with the cats and dogs. There wereabout 14 cats and 4 dogs. Our dogs' names were Taffy, Napoleon, Frenchy, and Fluffy.

That was three years of my living with Aunt Lillian and Uncle Duke, without seeing my mother very much, or my father – never, that I can remember. I guess that I just accepted the situation and went with the flow. As an eight, then nine-year-old, I just didn't **ask** many questions about the situation, and I am not sure why, to this day.

Well, my life was about to make a drastic change! In the summer of 1957 when I was 9 years old, and about to enter the fourth grade, my mother told me that Dad would have to continue to stay at the Veteran's Hospital in Miami, Florida, and that she and I were going to live with my grandmother and grandfather; Sphar and Patti Bruner, and Mom's mother; Sphar Bruner, Grandma's 3rd husband. They had relocated to Lexington, Kentucky from Wheelwright, Ky. My grandmother had been married before and outlived two husbands. Sphar was the brother of her second husband. Needless to say, the move took a lot of adjusting. Imagine moving from the country where you lived as a child with your cousins for three years with much family activity, playing, and interacting with everyone, then moving to a small city house on a very small lot, and with no children to play with. We lived at 133 Paris Court, now called Wittland Lane, in Lexington, Ky., and the house is still there today, but the shared garage at the end of the shared driveway has been torn down. I don't know why we didn't return to the house on Lincoln Avenue. **I never asked.**

House on Paris Court

My grandparents house had a living room, two small bedrooms, a kitchen with a small breakfast nook, one bathroom, plus a rear screened porch. Across the street were several houses next to a church. Later, those houses were torn down to make room for a larger church parking lot. At the back of one of the buildings were two basketball goals where I frequently shot hoops until I had my own basketball goal in our driveway. My grandfather was retired from the railroad as a train engineer, and my grandmother was a stay at home grandparent. However, Granddad had a night job until his final retirement. He was a security night watchman at Harry Gordon Scrap Yard in the city, which I will talk about later, as **it became an important place of discovery for me.** So that left just my grandma and me at the house at night. My mother and I shared the other bedroom. During this time, and until her retirement, Mom worked as a telephone operator for Shaw Answering Service. She would work third shift from 11-7AM, so I was always in bed before she went to work. When I was at school during the day Mom would sleep, but she was always awake when I got home from school.

Obviously, this move also meant that I was out of my old school district, and I had to attend a school in the city. Arlington Elementary School was three blocks from my house, and yes, I walked to school almost every day. Sometimes when it was raining Mom would drop me off at the side door on Avon Avenue beside the school.

I enjoyed the four years there at the school. The teachers were good. I still remember their names; Mrs. Richie, Mrs. Weinman, Miss Foster, and Mrs. Stein. I felt in place. It was a great environment for me during this time in my life. I will never forget the playground. When it was recess time, we could go out for 30 or 40 minutes of playtime! The playground had a sloping hill that seemed to go on forever, and we could go to the very back and hardly ever see the school. There was plenty of room for us to run around. One of the special things the boys did a lot was playing marbles. Children just don't do that anymore that I have seen. You find dirt spots on the ground and make a large circle. In the middle of the circle we would draw a line and make a little mound along the line. On top of that line we would put all our marbles in a row. Then we each took turns, one at a time, and with one marble locked between our thumb and finger, each player would try to shoot someone else's marble out of the circle. If there was success in doing this, that player got to keep the marble that he shot out of the circle. But on some occasions, some of us would bring a large marble two to three times the size of a regular marble, and these were our monster marbles. Not every student had one, but the guys that did had a distinct advantage in being able to knock multiple marbles out of the circle at one time. I had one, and it was a lot of fun taking my classmates marbles. They asked me where I got such a large marble. My response was truthfully, "I don't know. It just showed up at my house one day, and I found it in the garage." Of course, what would any playground be like without the monkey bars? We spent many happy minutes climbing those things, hanging around, swinging, and hanging upside down. What fun it was! After recess, as we returned to our classrooms, I still remember how long the hallways were with plenty of daylight coming in. I don't remember that we had lockers. It just seemed that we kept everything in our room.

Fourth grade was especially exciting for me. That is when I was officially introduced to a real shop. Can you imagine in this day and time letting fourth graders go into a real working woodshop which has saws and hammers, chisels and drills, and allowing your child to cut and make things from wood?

We would head down to the lower floor of the school. The woodshop was half above ground, and half below ground. There were windows halfway up on the outside wall. There must have been about 10 work benches in the shop with solid wooden tops, and with a vise attached to each bench. It was so much fun taking a saw and cutting a piece of wood, then shaping it; taking a chisel and cutting a groove in the wood so that pieces would fit together, taking a drill and drilling small holes, screwing things together. I still have a small rocking cradle, which was the very first thing I ever made in that shop! One day I will give it to my son or one of my grandchildren.

I still remember one of the special honors I had in the fourth grade. At least, I considered it an honor. We still had chalk blackboards and blackboard erasers in the classroom. Those erasers would always get full of chalk dust. I was selected by my teacher to be the official eraser cleaner. No, we did not have to take the erasers outside and bang them against the wall of the school building or bang the erasers against each other to clean off the chalk dust. Arlington Elementary School was high tech! We had a special eraser cleaning machine, and it was stored down in the mechanical room in the school's basement. I can remember going down into the lower area past our wood shop and opening a door, and then proceeding down a series of steps into that mechanical room; and there was the eraser cleaning machine! I would plug it in and turn the switch on. It was kind of like a vibrating sander, but it didn't sand. One at a time, I would take each eraser and run it across the top of the machine. It would pound the eraser. There was a vacuum underneath that would suck all the chalk dust into a bag. I was trusted to do this alone! I felt so important.

I really enjoyed my fifth grade class. It was on the second floor of the school building. My seat was on the outer row next to the windows. I would sit there during class and just look out the window, watching all the cars going by, daydreaming! I guess that's why my mother had to hire a tutor to help me learn the multiplication tables. Once or twice a week I would go over to my Aunt Nannie's house. My mother would drop me off, and a tutor would show up to help me with my multiplication lessons for about an hour. Then Mom would come and pick me up. In the fifth grade I got sent to the principal's office one time. I can't remember what I did, but I do remember getting lectured very seriously and shown a very large paddle that would be used on my backend, and if this ever happened again, I would feel the wrath of the paddle! Well, I never had to go back to the principal's office. That was a lesson well-learned!

Well, I graduated from the fifth grade to the sixth grade and got to move across the hall to Miss Foster's classroom. Miss Foster was a beautiful young teacher, and I think that was my first teacher-crush. Sixth grade was an interesting year. I was asked to do some things and **made some discoveries**. In history, each of us had to memorize something. This was the first time in my life I had to memorize a passage and present it orally to the class. Mine was the Gettysburg Address. I can remember still today standing in front of my classmates and reciting from memory the Gettysburg Address. And I got it all right, non-stop, from beginning to end.

The thing that I was asked to do that did cause some discomfort involved my penmanship. I have not told you until now, but I am left-handed. Well! Miss Foster tried to change my writing hand from left to right. She would put the pencil in my right hand, show me how to hold it, and then I had to practice writing script and writing the alphabet right-handed. Well, she quickly learned that this wasn't going to work, so she allowed me to rotate my paper, to grip my pencil with my left hand, and to continue writing left-handed. Looking back, I guess at the time it helped to develop a side of my brain that I hadn't used much before in that manner, so I guess I'm saying that I became mentally ambidextrous; right-brained and left-brained. To this day, some things I do left-handed and some things I do right- handed.

I thought I was having a great year in the sixth grade, but near the end of the school term, Miss Foster had a serious conversation with my mother. "Your son's year wasn't too bad. He is still weak in many subject areas. We can move him on into the seventh grade, but I think it would be better if he repeated the 6th grade because moving into seventh grade is a big adjustment academically, and he needs to be strong academically when that move takes place." Well, that conversation convinced my mother that I was going to repeat the six grade again. Ugh! I was not happy at all because my cousin Duke was now going to be a grade ahead of me. But the good news was that I got to spend much of the summer playing with Duke and my other cousins.

One thing I will never forget from that summer between sixth grade and sixth grade is an unwanted surprise from my cousin Becky. I think she had already surprised her brother Duke with the same unwanted gift, because they both meandered over to me in the yard, and Becky said, "Close your eyes and open your mouth. I want to give you a big surprise!" I thought it was going to be a candy treat or something like that because my cousin Becky was so sweet. So trustingly, I closed my eyes, opened my mouth, and she stuck a dandelion in my mouth. Yuck! They started laughing, as I began to spit out dandelion puffball seeds! I was not laughing at the time, but looking back now, it was a funny moment.

Summer was always a time for **discovery** and family activities, which, for the most part, included my cousins, my mother, my aunt and uncle, and me. Almost every Saturday or Sunday after church we went on mountain and lake outings. In the mountains we would visit the areas of the Red River Gorge. There, we traveled to places like Chimney Rock, Natural Bridge, Rock Bridge, and Sky Bridge.

Chimney Rock

Natural Bridge

Sky Bridge

Rock Bridge

These were all-natural geographical features, and some were state parks. We would hike many of the trails. Our parents would let us go ahead on the trails because they were obviously slower than us. We kids would run ahead. We always knew where the trails would take us because we had been on them many many times, sometimes passing other hikers. Usually, it was mostly our families on these ventures. After everyone completed the trails or activities, we would gather at the picnic tables for lunch, then drive back home by evening time. I still remember climbing on rocky ledges on those trips. We knew not to get too close to the edges for fear of falling. We were like true Kentucky mountain people exploring the territories.

We made other amazing summertime discoveries on our trips to the lake. We would pack up on Friday afternoon and head to Lake Cumberland. My uncle had a truck and a speedboat. He would attach the boat trailer to the truck, load up with camping supplies and food for the weekend, and we were off! There wasn't enough room for everyone to go in the truck, so we traveled in other vehicles as well. We were a mini caravan headed to the lake! Whenever we reached the campsite, the first thing we did was set up the tent. I do remember one trip we arrived after dark. It was pouring down rain, and we had to set the tent up in the rain. Needless to say, everyone was drenched! But the tent got set up. We built a campfire, the rain stopped, and everyone dried off. On these trips my cousins and I would roam through the woods, gather firewood, and enjoy all the water activities. We would go swimming, of course. We had inner tubes that we would sit on and float around on the lake. Of course, everyone went water skiing. We would do a lot of fishing, and I mean, we would do a lot of fishing! Sometimes we would be out in the boat all day fishing, come back, eat some dinner, then go out and do some night fishing. We would also boat into one of the lake coves and put out a trout line, which we would go back to, and check the next day. We did so much fishing as children, I think I got fished out! We would usually eat whatever we caught, and I mean, everything! Bass, crappie, catfish, and yes, even carp.

I never will forget our biggest fishing time. We were all fishing around a cove near our campground, and we must have been fishing in a school of crappie, because in about an hour's time, with about six of us fishing, we caught almost a hundred crappie! We did take some back home to put into the freezer for later eating. The thing I remember about being with my cousins and family is that all of us children were given a lot of freedom to explore and **discover** without being closely supervised by adults. On one of our lake trips my cousin Duke and I found a bunch of logs, big limbs, and some boards that had collected at the end of one of the coves. I thought, "Let's make a raft." Duke asked his dad if he had any rope, hammer, or nails. And, believe it or not, in his truck, he did have a hammer and nails. So, we waded into the water in the cove and started to build our Tom Sawyer raft. When we were finished, it was probably the ugliest looking raft anyone could imagine, but it floated, and Duke and I could stand on it without sinking. We pulled two long oars out of the boat, and we just paddled around in the cove on our raft. Our parents couldn't believe what we had just done! When we left the camp that weekend, we left the raft for someone else to navigate. In today's world it seems that children are not given the same responsibilities and freedoms as we had. Those experiences helped us to become independent, and to also rely on each other. We were **asking, discovering,** and **sharing**. There are many, many, more stories which could be told about our mountain and lake adventures, but the point is, on the weekends we got out of town as a family unit and spent time interacting with one another in God's great land. We all hated for summer to end because we had to return to school.

So, the summer was now over, and it was time to

repeat the sixth grade. My teacher would be Miss Stein. I learned that she was a new teacher at the school, and that she was of German descent. She was very strict, and she looked like she had a mustache, but it was just a little hair on her lip. Repeating sixth grade was so easy, and it did strengthen my academic skills, I guess, because I was reviewing what I had learned the year before. While I was in elementary school, home life was really good. I remember, however, that when I came home from school every day the very first thing I had to do was to finish my homework, and I could not go out and play until it was completed, no matter how long it took. On rare occasions, I would work on my homework until dinner time, then the next thing you know, it was time to get ready for bed. But most of the time I did have plenty of daylight playing time. There weren't a lot of kids on our street, maybe two. I did have a lot of freedom, though. I had a Cadillac of a bicycle.

My Huffy Bike

It was a Huffy Radio Bike! It actually had an AM and FM radio built into the bike and a big brick battery on the back to power it. Just imagine riding your bicycle while also listening to the radio. How cool was that! I never found another boy or girl that had one. I rode that bicycle everywhere around the neighborhood. But there was one exception. I never crossed the railroad tracks into "Irish Town", which is what we called it back then. It was a rough and tumble neighborhood with many run-down houses. Most often I would ride my bike up to Loudoun House on the grounds of Castlewood Park. This was a huge park with playground, baseball fields, and a large swimming pool. Loudoun House looked like a medieval castle.

The Castle

I could ride all over the place up there. On certain days I would ride up and watch the baseball games. On other days I would go and see what was going on in the gym. Sometimes I would just pull up by the swimming pool and watch the people swim, or I would ride the bike down the big hill in front of the swimming pool. It was a great place to bike and have fun. When I wasn't biking around Castlewood Park, I was cruising up and down the streets in our neighborhood.

When I wasn't riding around on the bicycle I was playing in the backyard. In the back-right corner of our yard I had a little log cabin playhouse that had a sandbox inside. I would go there for hours and build things in the sand. Our house had a shared driveway and a shared two car garage with a dividing wall between the two garage doors. On the side of the garage was a storage room/shop. There was a long built-in workbench with an operable shed window above. I would go out there and make playthings; wooden swords and toy guns, planes, etc., using whatever materials were available. I did discover that in the garage there was a cabinet where my grandfather Sphar kept the whisky hidden from his wife, Patti. I am not sure why, because Grandmother kept her whisky in the kitchen cabinet for "medicinal purposes". I **asked** myself a lot of things while playing in the garage alone, like, "What happens when you hold a match in front of a hair spray can, and you press the button?" Instant flame thrower! It's amazing that we survive our childhood! One time I was working in the shop, tripped and fell on a windowpane that was propped against the wall, and I still have the scar to this day from that adventure.

There were also moments that could have been terminal. One such incident was the day the neighborhood kids and I were playing "Hide-

and-Go-Seek". Yes, we finally had a few kids in the neighborhood. That particular day we decided to play on our street. It was late in the afternoon, and we all went to hide. It had rained earlier in the day, so everything was still wet. I decided to climb the sugar maple tree in our back yard and hide. I must have been well hidden because I stayed up in that tree until it started getting dark. No one could find me, and my friends all went home, so I started to climb down the tree. I was about fourteen feet up in the tree and on my descent, I slipped and fell back, headed toward the ground. I landed on top of our picket fence. Luckily, I hit the fence at an angle, or I would have been impaled. I knocked three pickets out of that fence, broke the fence, and ended up on the ground on my back! I thought I was in bad shape, as I could hardly breathe. The fall had knocked the breath clean out of me! I was able to turn over and crawl about ten feet to a concrete pad just outside our back door. There I lay for several minutes, gasping for air and moaning. Finally, my grandmother came out, and she was certainly startled. Her grandson was hurt, and under her watch. All she could really do was to try and comfort me with calming words as I regained my breath. She helped me into the house and to my bed. That week I went to the doctor, and all I had was a severely scraped, bruised, and sprained back. To me, that was my first near death experience. Later in life there were two others which will be revealed later.

Then there were those magnificent discovery

nights when I was asked if I would like to spend the night at work with Mom or Granddad. If you recall, I mentioned that my mother worked at a telephone answering service. The service was referred to as the Physician's Exchange. This was a special business that catered to doctors in the medical profession in Lexington, Kentucky. Doctors could purchase a phone number to be used when they were out of the office or too busy to answer their office phone. During this time in history everyone was still using the rotary telephone. Everyone had individual single lines. I will never forget the first time I went to my mom's office in the evening to spend the night. In the room where she worked, there were several tables that had hundreds of telephones on them, and each one was an individual rotary phone. During the night the phone would ring, and my mother had to identify which phone was ringing before she picked up the receiver. When my mother answered the phone, she was in communication with the doctor or someone who wanted to speak with a doctor. She took messages, and those messages were relayed later to the physician's office. I can close my eyes to this day see all those telephones. I don't know how she kept track of everything, but she was very efficient. So good at what she did! I would eventually be sent to the front office which had some desks and a sofa. There was a window that overlooked the old post office. The sofa became my bed for the night, and it was quite comfortable. I was content and warm, staying there with my mother at the office.

Down the hall from Mom's office was a dentist's office. I don't know if my mother got a discount because she knew the dentist, but that's where I went for my early dental work. I never liked going there. It was like going to a torture chamber, but I was given some novocaine. For me, it was never enough! I can still hear the grinding drill bits on my teeth to this day. I still never want to go to the dentist because of those early experiences. There were many times that I was able to go and spend the evening and be with my mom at work. She would always have paper and pencil for me, so I could sketch and draw, and doodle. I guess that's when I really started drawing.

Since I mentioned drawing, there was one thing at my grandma's house that I saw which led me to **ask** something that led to a **discovery**. I was in my bedroom one day, and I saw an object laying up against the wall. It was a strange looking device, and it actually looked like a pick hammer. I asked my mother what it was, and she said it was a T-Square. "What's it used for?" I asked. She replied, "It's used to make drawings, and it's used on a flat board to help you draw straight lines." I was really intrigued. When I saw drawings that had been made with this T-square, I wanted to do the same thing. That began my asking, "What is architecture?" I think I wanted to be an architect at that moment! I was in the fifth or sixth grade at the time. Even today when I reflect on that event, I still do not know why that T-square was in our house, let alone, in my bedroom.

Other great evening **discovery** times were spent with my grandfather at the junkyard. Grandpa was the night watchman there. Grandma would always fix dinner for Grandpa to take with him because he worked all night at the junkyard. On nights that I would spend there with him, my mother would drive me and drop me off around 5 or 6:00 p.m. I would spend the whole night there, and then she would come and pick me up in the morning just before the business reopened again. This was an amazing place for me, as a young boy, to experience. It was just my grandfather and me, there at the junkyard. I had free reign over the entire place. It was my "Junkyard Kingdom". I could go out and explore, and what an amazing place for me to explore! There were piles of scrap metal everywhere, and they were separated according to the types of metal. There were piles of aluminum, steel, iron, and copper. There were big machines that could grind and mash a car into metal bales of metal scrap about the size of straw bales. I remember looking down into the pit of one of those machines when it was empty and thinking I would never want to fall into that. At the junkyard there was also a railroad line. There were always box cars lined up. Most of the box cars were empty when I was there, and I got to climb up into the box cars and explore the inside all by myself. Grandpa let me have this freedom, I think, because there were microphones planted all around the scrap yard, and he could listen inside the office at night to determine if there were any intruders who had entered the business. He would continually remind me, "If you need something, just shout out, and I will hear you." Grandpa always took his 12-gauge shotgun with him to work. I guess that was part of his security responsibilities.

One evening I was walking around the scrap yard with my grandfather, and he was carrying the 12-gauge shotgun. We stopped, and he looked down at me and said, "Herbie, do you want to shoot the shotgun?" What young boy would say "No", so he handed me the 12-gauge shotgun, and it was all I could do just to hold the barrel up straight because it was heavy. The shotgun had two triggers, one for each barrel. My grandfather said, "See that open metal safe over there?" It was about 30 or 40 feet in front of me. "See if you can shoot inside that safe." Well, I pulled that trigger, and the next thing I knew I was picking myself up off the ground! My grandfather was laughing because when I pulled the trigger, the recoil made me pull the other trigger at the same time, and I had shot both barrels at once! I looked around for the shotgun and it was not in my hands! It was lying about six feet away from me and had breached itself open.

Grandpa continued to laugh! It was really a very memorable experience, and I will never forget it. Since then, I have learned how to shoot a shotgun without it knocking me down. As I mentioned earlier, what an amazing place the junk yard was for me to explore! There was a building I could enter where the daytime employees would take machines apart so they could recycle the scrap materials. I got to see the inside mechanisms of so many devices, and it was amazing! I was able to see how gears made machines work, to see electronic devices which still had electronic tubes in them, to see coin-operated vending machines, and to **discover** how they worked. One thing I really liked about the vending machines is that they had magnets in them to catch coins that were counterfeit. Grandpa let me take the magnets out of any machine that I could find, and needless to say, I had the largest magnet collection of any boy in the city, of all shapes and sizes. So I was able to see the end results of things that were made by the great minds in our country, and I was given an opportunity to take things apart which let me to begin seeing how reverse engineering works.

Then, there were those special **asking, discovering,** and **sharing** moments with my grandmother in the evenings when we were the only ones at home, because her husband, Sphar, and her daughter, my mother, worked at night. When it was time to begin to get ready for bed, I would put on my pajamas and go to Grandma's bedroom for evening radio time. On cold days she would light the gas heater, and I would lay on the floor in front of it, gazing in amazement, looking at the long horizontal row of flames that were being created to heat the room. It was almost hypnotic. While I lay there, we would listen to radio shows, like "Amos and Andy". I will never forget King Fish because of his unique voice, Then there was "Adventures of Superman", "The Lone Ranger", "Sparky", "Dick Tracey", and many more. As I listened, my mind would create visual images of what I was hearing. Those radio shows took my mind to so many places that I only envisioned. I never really read many books, so this was the primary way I "saw" things that others read about. On those cold evenings, my grandmother would put a brick on top of the gas heater to heat and later use to warm her feet when she went to bed. She had this peculiarly shaped white sock that she put the brick in, and it looked so strange. I remember asking her one night why that sock looked so strange. She said, "Well, if someone lost their leg at the knee, this is the kind of sock they would wear to give them comfort, and it's the perfect size to hold my brick." I never asked anymore about that sock!

Grandma was my go-to person most of the time. I really loved my grandmother, even though she could be stern at times. During the day, my mom and grandfather would be sleeping because of their night work. So, I had to be quiet in the house or go out and play. Sometimes Grandma and I would catch the bus at the end of our street, ride down to Main Street, and go to the movies. We usually went to the Strand Theater or the Ben-Ali Theater in Lexington, Kentucky. After the movie we would walk home, and at the time I thought it was a long walk. Being curious,

I recently measured the distance on google earth, and it was less than 2 miles!

Grandma was the chief cook and bottlewasher at home, and she could really cook well! Before my grandparents moved to Lexington my mom was still a child. I was told that Grandma used to cook for the railroad workers up in the mountains of Kentucky. She would prepare meals for hundreds of people.

Her cooking and canning skills also led us to have many family country outings. We would go to Kerry's farm in Indian Old Fields outside of Winchester, Kentucky, to pick blackberries. It was primitive. Kerry lived in an old log house on the farm, and he would let us "have at it" in the blackberry fields! Those wild blackberries were growing everywhere. We would go there with my cousins and my aunt and uncle, spending the day picking blackberries. Man, O man, did we ever pick blackberries! We filled bucket after bucket until the big metal wash tub was filled. If Kerry had recently plowed the fields, Duke and I would look for arrowheads. We had no problem finding them. They seemed to be everywhere. We were told that the area had been a great hunting ground for the Native Americans centuries earlier, and I believed it!

Well, when the blackberries made their way back to our house, my grandmother would start making her famous blackberry jam. She would prepare gallons and gallons of jam, fill up mason jars for families. The word would leak out, and strangers would show up at the house for jam. Like I said, she was a great cook!

Also, when the word got out that she was making her custard, relatives would drive down from Cincinnati to take some back home with them for Christmas.

I was now in the sixth grade the second time, and it was a most uneventful year, with one exception. My mother introduced me to the Boy Scouts. Previously, I had been a Cub Scout in my mother's Den. My Boy Scout Troop met at a church just a few blocks away from my elementary school. I **discovered** in scouting that it was my responsibility to honor God and my country. I learned the correct way to walk, feet parallel with toes pointing straight ahead, and to walk straight and upright. I earned a few merit badges, made it to First Class, but I never advanced beyond that, and I'll tell you why in a little bit. The most exciting thing for me in Boy Scouts was that we could volunteer to be ushers at the University of Kentucky home basketball games. We were given a patch armband and had to wear our uniform when we went to the games. My mother would drop me off at the basketball games, where I would help usher people to their seats. I was able to watch all of the famous Kentucky basketball games as a young boy. I got to see Cotton Nash, Pat Riley, and "Pistol Pete" Maravich! That's when I really developed a love for basketball. As it turned out, my cousin Ray was still at the University, majoring in art, and he was also one of the male cheerleaders for the University of Kentucky. After the games were over, I would go down to cousin Ray, and he would take me home. Sometimes he would drop some cheerleaders off at the dorm or stop and talk with one of his girlfriends. To me, it seemed that he was very popular on campus!

Well, six grade, "Round 2", was over, and during those two years I had a growth spurt. I haven't mentioned until now that in the fourth and fifth grade sometimes when I walked to school, I would be bullied along the way by some of those kids that lived in Irish Town across the railroad tracks from my house. When that growth spurt hit, I was now looking down at those little kids who used to bully me; "little kids", because I had outgrown them so much, they seemed like little kids to me. I never had any more trouble from them! My school life was about to transition dramatically. It was now time for me to enter **Junior High School!**

There was still a little time left in summer before I started Junior High School, and there was something on my mind that I just had to **ask** about to see if I could get more clarity. Why was my dad not around? So, **I asked the big question!** "Tell me about Dad, and why does he have to be in the hospital in Miami?" I guess Mom felt that I was now old enough and mature enough to hear the truth. Believe me, it was a shock when I heard the story! Mom told me that when we were living on Lincoln Avenue, and I was a young infant, my father had returned home from WW II. He had been working in military intelligence. He had seen some horrific things and had participated in some horrific things while working. I don't know how long he had been home, but as Mom told the story, one day she was in the kitchen and heard me crying loudly in another room. Then the crying seemed to stop immediately, which was unusual. She hurried to the room where she found my father pressing a pillow over my face, smothering me, as he was trying to get me to stop crying. Mom said that when Dad saw her, he looked shocked and seemed to be in a daze. He removed the pillow immediately, and then he realized what he had done.

I was so young that I don't remember any of it. It seems that my dad had PTSD. Back then, no one knew what to call it and how to treat it. Later, realizing that he could have taken my life, it was just too much stress. Sometime later, I don't know exactly when, he took his service revolver and shot himself in the head. His suicide attempt did not kill him. He was rushed to the hospital and survived. He eventually had to be taken to the Veteran's hospital in Miami for additional treatment where they had to put a metal plate in his head. Doctors said that it was a medical miracle that he survived. They had never seen anyone live from a wound to the head like his. Finally, I had an answer! Now I knew why my mother wanted me to go and live with my aunt and uncle, allowing her to deal with my dad's situation for three years, on and off, in Miami.

Sometime later, I found out that my dad was going through rehabilitation at the same hospital in Miami. Because of the rehabilitation program, he was permitted to return to Lexington occasionally. On one of those return visits my mother found him in our bathroom with his hands around my throat. I guess I was making too much noise, and it was disturbing to him. Apparently, his rehabilitation for PTSD was not working as well as planned. It was at that time in our family life that my mother realized there had to be a separation between us and Dad. Looking back now, I realize I was never told, but that's probably the reason we went to live my grandparents. I'm sure it was. Mom still stayed in touch with Dad, keeping track of his progress, but our family was now separated permanently.

Looking back now, I cannot even begin to think how difficult the situation was for my mother. She was loving her son and trying to make sure he was in the safest and most enriching environment he could be in with family. At the same time, she was still trying to care for my father. It brings me to tears as I reflect on how she tried to care for me and the love she gave me. Mom was like an angel to everyone. She was like a mother figure to everyone. The following scriptures describe some of the qualities of my mother.

> *Proverbs 31 v25 "She is clothed with strength and dignity; she can laugh at the days to come."*

> *Philippians 4 v13 "I can do all things through him who strengthens me."*

Proverbs 22 v6 "Start children off on the way they should go, and even when they are old, they will not turn from it."

Proverbs 31 v15-17 "She gets up while it is still night; she provides food for her family. She sets about her work vigorously; her arms are strong for her tasks."

My cousin, Ray, who was at UK, would come over to our house and just hang out and share his problems with my mom. Sometimes it's easier to share with someone other than your parents and seek advice. If you went to Mom's house and made a comment about something beautiful you saw there, I don't know, a little vase, or perhaps a decorative plate, she would   just say, "Why don't you take that home with you?" Material things didn't mean that much. It was those intangible things that meant a lot, like love, friendship, and helping others. That's why it's so important to start **asking, discovering,** and **sharing** those important times in your family life, and to discover by sharing, that you may impact important times in the lives of others. Its not only important to share, but it's even more important to be an example for others to learn from and to follow.

One such example of her loving-kindness occurred about 20 years into my marriage. It involved something that I had no knowledge of. My mother had passed many years earlier and is now in Heaven.

So, one day it was about 8:00 in the evening, and my wife and I were winding down from a busy day. The phone rang, and when I answered the voice said, "This is John. We went to High School together. Do you remember me?" I think I did, but vaguely. "You might not be aware of this, but at one time my wife worked with your mother at the Physician's Exchange. She told your mother about our engagement, and that she did not have enough money to buy me a wedding band."

My mother had said, "Not to worry. Things will work out." Later, my mom gave her my dad's wedding band and told her that she could give it to her future husband on the day they were married. So, John was calling me to let me know that his wife had recently passed away due to cancer, and he told me the story about the wedding band. He asked me if I'd like to have my father's wedding band. I was overcome with surprise and said, "Absolutely!" So, he put it in the mail, and several days later I received my father's wedding band with his name on the inside of it. That's just one example of how great, caring, and loving my mother was to others. This is a story that I share with many now, and I will in the future, so that they, too, may discover what sharing really means when it comes from the heart. To this day, I have my dad's wedding band stored in a safe and special place to be shared some time in the future.

So, let us return to the story "time-line". I was now ready for junior high school. It seemed that where I was living at the time on Paris Court would put me into the Lexington Junior High School District. My mother thought it would be better if I could go to Junior High School where my cousins went. So, she told "the powers that be" in the school district that my home address, or better, my mailing address, was 147 Winston Avenue which is also where one of my other cousins lived; Gladys Louise Allison. That address was almost adjacent to the school grounds of Bryan Station. So, everything worked out. I started junior high at Bryan Station, the same school where I attended grades one through three. But now Bryan Station was no longer an elementary school, but just a junior high school. I was returning to a familiar environment, but there would be new faces and new people, other than just my cousin Duke, to interact with. If you recall, I was introduced to the sport of basketball as a Boy Scout usher at the home games, and I also had a sudden growth spurt and had developed a passion for basketball. So, it seemed inevitable that I try out for the basketball team. I was about 6'3" tall at the time. I made the team and continued to play basketball every year until I graduated. I also played one year of football and was on the track team in high school, participating in field events; discus, shotput, long jump, etc..

I was still too young to drive, so my mother would take me to school in the morning, drop me off, and pick me up when school was out in the afternoon. When basketball season came, it really took up a lot of free time, but I was doing something I loved! My junior high school basketball coach's name was.

Mr Handcock. He asked the players on the team just to call him "Coach", but for some reason I couldn't. Out of respect I always call him Mr. Hancock.

Mom would pick me up after practice, and sometimes she would stay and talk a few minutes with a coach. I never knew what they talked about. I was always ready just to get home after a hard day's practice. Then when basketball season was over, I was **asked** something that was interesting! Mr. Hancock had mentioned to my mother that he and his wife worked in the summer at a sports camp in Sebring, Florida. He asked my mother if I might also be interested in working there as a junior counselor. What boy in his right mind would say "No"! Give up an opportunity to spend 6 weeks in Florida and participate in teaching sports? What a dream job! Although it didn't pay anything, that was okay. I had a place to sleep, free food, and I could teach others all kinds of sporting activities!

Children at the camp ranged in age from first grade to sixth grade. So, for three years during the summer, Mr. Don Hancock became a father figure to me and all through junior high school, as my basketball coach. I am so thankful now that I had his fatherly influence in my life at a time when I could have chosen a different path that might have led to pain and suffering because of bad decisions. Because of respect for him and his wife, I never wanted to let them down.

The camp was called "Camp Sparta". There were about a dozen cabins for the boys and girls to stay in, I think six for the boys and six for the girls. My first year I was in a cabin with about eight children, ages 6-8 years old. Each cabin had an adult counselor and a junior counselor. I was a junior counselor, and the counselor in the cabin with me was Larry Langan. Larry was a student at Transylvania University and a baseball player there, as well (Larry eventually became a lawyer, and later a district attorney in Kentucky). His brother, Tommy, was also a junior counselor at camp and played basketball at the Catholic High School in Lexington. We were high school basketball rivals, but teammates as junior counselors at camp. So, try to imagine. Larry and I were in the cabin with these young children that had been dropped off for summer camp.

For many, it was their first time away from home and, oh boy, did some of them get home sick and cry for their parents! We would try to comfort them and help them write letters home to their parents. This was a season of leadership and **discovery** for me, but I did not realize it at the time. We had to ask the children to keep their beds made up and to keep their belongings picked up. We woke them up in the morning, took them to breakfast, saw them off to their activities, and then later took them back to the cabin so they could prepare for lunch. Then we escorted them to lunch, carted them back to the cabin after lunch for rest time, to afternoon activities, dinner, and then, to evening activities, and finally, back to the cabin for bed at night. There were beds provided in the cabin for Larry and me. You might say we were their only family during the summer. We were the ones who comforted them if they cried. We were the ones who continued to be their family during their stay at the camp. I wonder today if any of those campers remember us. We were **asked** to care and to teach others, and we **discovered** that we could do it quite well. No telling what I would have gotten into back home as a teenager during those three summers! Thanks, Larry, for being a mentor to me, and thanks, Mr. Handcock, for being a father figure to me!

Junior high school was a memorable time for me. There were basketball games, and there were sock hops in the gym in the evenings, which I really enjoyed because those were times that the students could mingle casually with one another. We had a great social time, dancing and talking with everyone. That's where real high school friendships started for me. I mentioned being introduced to shop and making things. That continued in junior high school. Our shop class was in a metal Quonset hut, detached from the main building. I always enjoyed learning how to make things from raw materials. Sometimes, now, when I am teaching a marketing class in Ukraine, I will give the students in my class a ball of clay and ask them to take something and make something. Then the next day I can see the creations that came from their minds and hands. I guess that's because I was influenced by my architectural academic environment where I took an idea of something and created something, for example, a building design. To this day, I still have the baseball bat that I made in my junior high school shop class, waiting to be shared with someone in the future. I cannot begin to imagine why we do not have shop classes for students in all grades in today's world. Shop classes helped my mind develop. These classes awaken the senses and certainly allow for creativity through hands-on experiences. I guess you might say I was just an average student all the way through junior high school and senior high school, but later when I **discovered** my passion more and more, I was able to excel. The Lord God was working in my life through my feeble **asking, discovering,** and **sharing**. There are many more stories to be told regarding my high school days, but for now I will save them for another time.

Also, as I look back on this section about family and school, I have many things that I wish I had **asked** about, but for some reason or another I didn't **ask**. I have compiled a list of things that I should have **asked** my parents, relatives, and teachers, but didn't. I hope this list will encourage you to start your own **asking, discovering,** and **sharing**. Begin by asking these questions to your parents, grandparents, and great grandparents, and record your answers:

Where are your grandparents originally from?
How did your grandparents meet?
Did your grandparents have any brothers or
  sisters?
What kind of work did you do?
Did you go to college?

Where was your home?

What was your house like?

Did you have a car? What kind?

Did anyone in the family serve in the military?

Did anyone have to go to war?

What do you remember as your happiest moments?

What was your saddest time?

What was technology like then?

What was the funniest thing that happened to you?

Where were you born?

What did you do for fun?

Did you have any pets?

Where have you traveled?

Did you have any chores?

What were the holidays like?

What do you recall about family gatherings?

What was your school like?

Who was your best friend?

Where did you get married, and when?

Tell me about your faith.

What were birthdays like?

What was your favorite book?

What did you see when you looked out the window?

What were your hobbies?

Did you do anything that got you into trouble?

How were you disciplined?

Have you met anyone famous?

Were you ever in the news?

What are your proud of?

What advice would you give me?

Those are the questions that came to my mind, and you may have others. You can also look on the internet and find many more questions to ask. But what has stood out to me is the relationship of togetherness, support, and success in a family. The next illustration shows the connectivity and interlocking aspect of those elements.

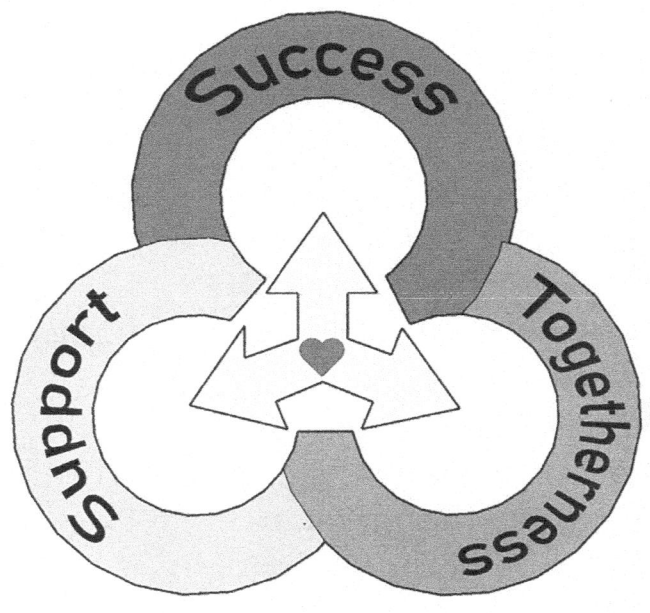

Remember as you continue reading that it is what is in your heart that affects your family, your work, and your faith.

When thinking about togetherness, that one word means "family" to me. In my life it was not only immediate family, but extended family; my mother, aunt, uncle, cousins, grandmother, and grandfather. Also, there is the togetherness that can be brought about through the loving kindness of others, as was exhibited by my basketball coach and his wife, and their influence on my life during my formative years. I hope one day that their children will discover if they have not already done so, the impact that their parents had on others.

Being together and having support is essential in families. It can be the energy from others that inspires you. Support can help to get you back on your feet from an injury or failure that has occurred within your family. Support is that arm around you or that loving hug, encouraging you.

Success seldom comes alone. When you look at successes in a family, they are usually a result of togetherness and/or support. Success is the result of your achieving your goals or completing the task at hand. Your success can become an example for others in your family. It can give you confidence to connect with and to motivate others.

The important thing is to start **asking** how to begin your new life of family discoveries so that you can share them and pass them on to other family members. Start today. **Ask, discover, and share!**

Hebrews 13 v16 "And do not forget to do good and to share with others, for with such sacrifices God is pleased."

Proverbs 3 v27 "Do not withhold good from those to whom it is due, when it is in your power to act."

CHAPTER THREE

Work

Work, work, work. What an incredible and amazing word this is! Consider the meaning of the word, "work", and look to the dictionary for an answer. It is striking that there are two important categories for the use of the word, "work". First the noun; "an activity involving mental or physical effort done to achieve a purpose or result"; then the verb; "a task or tasks to be undertaken". In the context of this book, the word "work" is the engine that can materialize and make functional the results of **asking**, **discovering**, and **sharing**.

Think about this for a moment. Have there been times when you had to work yourself up to the point where you were finally ready and prepared to ask someone something? **Asking** does require work, and more often than not, the results of **asking**, in some cases, will actually produce more work for you or work for others to do. Or it can cause you to cease working currently at/or with something. In the same light, the words "working" and "**discovery**" seem to join together. You can't have one without the other. And let's not forget the work involved with **sharing**. Just like **asking**, sometimes you have to work yourself up to be prepared to **share** with someone. I reflect back on the many presentations I have given and the tremendous amount of work that was involved in preparing those presentations.

Some people, including myself, at one time or another in their life, work hard not doing something they should be doing. Sometimes it might be intentional and other times there might be the moment when you are working so hard at something else that you really forget what the important work in life really means, and the impact that it can have on your future, and on others. Time is lost, and as you well know, it is time that can never be regained. It is so important in life that you discover what your passion is, and that you have a pathway vision through work to make your passion vision become a part of your everyday life. Don't misunderstand what I'm saying. Be very aware that passion and vision have to be able to sustain you physically, financially, and emotionally. Don't confuse this with a hobby, which is usually something you do in your spare time for personal enjoyment. When talking about work, I mean life-sustaining work that can affect those you love, those you work with, and other people you encounter in life.

Have you ever **asked** yourself these questions? What was it in life; when was it in life that affected your pathway? What decisions affected what you wanted to become in life? What was it that got you there, or continued to guide you? If you recall, for me there was that "aha" moment when I saw this strange looking object in my bedroom that looked like a pickaxe. I don't know how or why it was there, but when I found out it was a T-Square, and that it was used to create drawings for others to build things from, like architectural structures designed by architects, it was then, at an early age, that I knew I wanted to become an architect. Well, that pathway was a long and winding road, with barriers that developed along the way.

The first obstacles and opportunities concerning architecture occurred in junior high and senior high school. I will never ever forget that first obstacle when someone or something disagreed with what I wanted to do. I think it was in the eighth grade, and all the students had the opportunity to take this wonderful career survey which would reveal the best career path for us to consider in the future. I remember the survey was lengthy. It seemed like there were about a hundred questions we had to answer. It was a few days later that we got the survey results back. Mine were totally shocking! The results indicated that the best career path for me to pursue would be that of a forest ranger. What!? I was shocked and devastated! I guess all the survey questions that I answered were influenced by the many wonderful times our family spent in the outdoors; camping, hiking, water skiing, etc.. In my mind, I had determined to be an architect-yeah! And I didn't care what any survey would say about that, in trying to suggest that I might consider another profession. Naturally, I felt that the assessment was the first obstacle in my path.

The first opportunity occurred when I was a senior in high school. In our community we had vocational training for high schoolers. My high school counselor mentioned that there was a program in another high school in town, and if students from my school were interested in participating, they could do so. One of the vocational programs was technical drafting, which meant for the first time I would now be able to take a class and actually use that thing called a T-Square. So, I signed up to take the class that year. There were less than a dozen students from my school who participated. After our morning class, we would hop on a school bus and ride across town, eating our lunch as we traveled. Then our vocational training classes began! It was wonderful! I could now begin to learn how to draw mechanical designs, as well as architectural drawings for buildings. My instructor was Mr. Thompson, and he was the first black teacher that I had. He was excellent, knowledgeable, and he was also an encourager. If I had drawn something incorrectly, he would challenge me to think of his lessons and demonstrations regarding correct two-dimensional communication. I was able to create a modest portfolio from some of my class projects.

When a class ended, we would head to the bus for the trip back to our home high school. At school, we arrived in time for the last bell. Then I could go to basketball practice, and then track practice in the spring. That special time in by senior year encouraged me to continue my journey towards architecture, and it also fueled my love for basketball, which would later be my demise.

Wow! Senior year was over, graduation was behind, and I felt free at last! Now with all that freedom, came the responsibilities of the present and the future, summer work, then college at the University of Kentucky as an architecture major, and a beginning of the fulfillment of my dreams. My cousin Ray had worked at a place called Cormans Inc. for many years, and his best friend, Dwight, married my cousin Becky. Dwight had a lead design position in the company. I was able to get a job there in the summer between my junior and senior year of high school and the summer after graduation. What an amazing place to work! It was like Santa's Workshop. At Cormans they designed anything you could imagine for special events, retail environments, Christmas decorations for department stores, etc.; like creating Santa castles-full size, and multi-story structures from cardboard, and light framing materials. I learned how to take cardboard and make what looked like, from a distance, a real brick veneer wall; how to make a boat from cardboard for displays, and how to gold leaf. For special events we would go to Keeneland Racetrack and hang bunting from the roof trusses for July 4th celebrations, or we would go to a nearby horse farm and decorate for a derby party.

I will never forget one time when the venue for a party was to be around a pool at a horse farm. First, we inflated about 100 balloons, then put them in the pool and covered the balloons with a cloth net that we weighted down, so that the balloons would stay under the water. They would be released at a later time and float to the surface. Then we cut 20 Styrofoam lily pads and attached big round candles to the pads so they could be lit and just float around in the pool. When I was asked to help, Dwight wanted to know if I wanted to jump into the pool to assist with the setup. Of course, being a young teenager, I said "Sure." Well! I was not told that the water in the pool was supplied from a local spring nearby. I discovered quickly how cold spring water is, and what I thought would be a fun thing to do, literally turned out to be a chilling experience. There are many more stories to share, but in keeping with the theme of this book, I was asked to build many decorative assemblies, others shared with me the processes and materials to use, and I **discovered** that I could produce creative works required for my job. Those skills and learning experiences became useful many times later in my life.

Summer was ending. It was 1967, and little did I know that I was really beginning to discover what real work was all about. I have continued to do so for many more years into my 60's and early 70's. In high school I considered myself an average student academically, and an above average athlete.

At the University, I was signed up for all of the prerequisite classes like English, History, Psychology, etc., those classes that would lead to fun classes in my major. I was in college, and the reality of work began to set in.

Work a job to make car payments
Work to make good grades
Work to make friends
Work at having fun (playing around)
Work at not failing
Work should be fun
Work should not be hard
Work at being good in life
Work at keeping your faith (especially in college)
Work at planning your future
Work for the love of someone

Classes had started, and I was now a student of architecture at the university. I was free from the regulated structure and accountability of high school. Free to go and come as I pleased. Free to make decisions for myself. Do you remember that moment in your life?

Fall semester had just started, and I discovered two incredible opportunities in the first few weeks. First, I discovered the Student Union, and second, tryouts for the UK Freshman Basketball Team! The Student Union was an incredible place in a large cafeteria. There were areas where students could go in rooms and study alone. There were large lounging areas with tables and chairs to play cards and hang out, and, oh yes! There was the billiards room! I spent a lot of time there. All you had to do was show them your student ID card and play as long as you wanted to. I did become a pretty good pool player and card player because that was something I was working hard to do, not that it was going to help me in the future. It was just one of those things that are categorized as work for fun. I made some good friends, and every week for one or two days we worked hard at maintaining a regular card-playing time.

The other thing I worked quite hard at was playing basketball. I tried out for the Freshman Basketball Team at the University of Kentucky. During tryouts there were about 75 young men who wanted the chance of making the team. That year there were only four scholarship basketball players on the freshman team, so they had to fill in the gap. Well, after tryouts, to my shock and surprise, I was selected as one of the members of the UK Freshman Basketball Team. I think it was at that time in Kentucky that every boy had a dream of playing basketball at the University of Kentucky. I was now really high! I was working hard to excel in every practice and was holding my own with the others on the team. However, my work for fun and work for play took it's toll in other areas. As a result, I did not work hard in my classes, and I did not even care about making good grades. I must have been living in a dream world. My basketball career did not last long because when midterm grades were posted, mine were so low that I was asked to leave the Freshman Basketball Team. What a failure I was! I had worked so hard to accomplish one thing and worked so little to accomplish another. When grades were finally posted for the first semester, I think there was only one class that I passed, an art class. Sometimes we discover lessons that are really hard to learn, and I guess for me, my head was just too hard at this time in my life. After Christmas break the University allowed me to sign up for another load of classes for the spring semester, and then for the following fall semester. It was during my sophomore year that two things drastically changed in my life, one for the good and one for the worse.

The good thing that happened to me was on a rainy February day in 1969 at the Student Union. I had my lunch tray in my hand, and I began to look for a place to sit down and eat. I was by myself.

That particular day the eating area was crammed with many students, and there were very few places to sit.

I observed a table where no one was sitting at the time, but I did see three women's raincoats hanging on the backs of the chairs. I said to myself, "I think I'll sit down at that table and see who shows up, and if any of these women want me to leave when they come to the table, I will do so." Well, shortly thereafter three women did show up, and I was awestruck by one of them. She looked like Hayley Mills, the movie actress. I'm sure these girls were shocked to see a young man sitting at their table when they arrived, but they sat down with me anyway. We struck up a conversation and introduced ourselves. We had a great lunch time. The woman that I was starstruck with, well, I guess you could say it was love at first sight. Soon after, on February 14, 1969 we had our first date, and we eventually got married, 2 1/2 years later, and I'm still with my lovely wife of almost 49 years. God's angel was sent to me.

Now, what happened for the worse is that I continued to work hard at not being successful academically. So, at the end of the spring semester when the time came to register for the next semester classes. Sadly, I was informed by my advisor that I could not continue my education at the University of Kentucky. I was also told that I would have to leave the university for at least one year, perhaps go to another school, establish some better grades, and then I could try later to enroll again. "Woe is me! What now?" I thought. I had to find a job for the summer, find another school to go to, and I didn't want to screw things up with this beautiful young lady I was dating. This young woman turned my life around. I did not want to fail anymore because that might cause me to lose her. My love for her totally changed my work mentality.

I saw an ad in the newspaper that a local engineering firm, R. W. Booker and Associates, needed a draftsman. In high school I had created a small portfolio of drafting projects from my vocational training. I applied, showed them my work, and by the grace of God, I got the job, knowing I was a college flunk out!!. I am still amazed today, and realize now that God does have a plan for each of us. I **discovered** engineering processes for highway design, and was able to work on the Cave Run Reservoir in Kentucky. Later, I was assigned to assist the planner in charge, and we worked on city planning studies for several small towns in our state, creating neighbor analysis and town maps. Remember, a college flunky got to **discover** how to do these things. It's just incredible!

While I was working with them, I was desperately trying to locate somewhere else to go to school so I could eventually try and fulfill my vision of becoming an architect. Someone mentioned to me that they thought there was a Presbyterian junior college that might accept me, and the name was Lee's Junior College in Jackson, Kentucky. I applied, and to my surprise, I was accepted. It was a mountain college. My Kentucky friends can tell you what it was like in Jackson, and the other areas likes Whitesburg and Hazard, Kentucky; moonshining, and mountain family principals. If they don't know you, then you are a foreigner to them and have to earn their trust.

There are a lot of stories to tell from my one and a half years there:

- Spelunking with my professors
- The many gallons of moonshine in the dorm rooms (I was afraid to drink it)
- Washing dishes to pay for my tuition
- The dorm being shot up by a soldier home on leave because the black basketball players were dating the local girls
- My 16-year-old banjo picking National Champion, roommate, Raymond McClain
- My second dorm which used to be a mortuary
- My roommate driving my car off a cliff
- Having a gun pointed to my head (I could feel the end of the barrel against my head)
- Other stories, too many to mention

I would arrive usually on Sunday evening, stay on campus all week, and return to Lexington on Friday afternoon or evening. Did I mention there was not much to do? Really, there wasn't. Most of the evenings were spent in the dorm rooms studying and working on projects. Now that I had a love in my life, I did not want to fail. I began to really be serious about **asking**, **discovering**, and **sharing** all things academically, and contributing to college life there. It became the spark

I needed to move forward. That spark turned into a flame as I made the dean's list academically, became the president of our class, and graduated with an Associates Degree from Lee's Junior College. Also, I met two great lifelong friends, Vicki and Charlie. I personally introduced them to each other, and later they married. To this day we remain great friends.

Also, while I was attending Lee's Junior College, I continued to date the beautiful young woman, Susan, who I met in the college grill on my way out of the University. As we dated, our love grew for each other. I proposed to her, we got married the summer after my graduation from Lee's. All this time Susan pursued her dream of being an elementary school teacher. She had only two years left to get her bachelor's degree when I returned to the University of Kentucky. I was so blessed to have someone to **ask** things with, to **discover** things with, and to **share** visions and plans together for our futures.

Yes, I still wanted to be an architect. Now it was time for me to shift gears and try to get admitted back into the University of Kentucky with a major in Architecture, which was a five year professional degree program. Well, as I mentioned earlier, God has a plan for everyone. I contacted the University about re-admittance. As it turned out that year, a special academic policy was instituted, and it was called Academic Bankruptcy. If a student once attended the university, left, and had not taken any classes there for at least one year, if re-admitted, their academic record would be wiped clean! What that meant is that in any previous classes taken, whatever grade was earned in those classes would not be calculated into the grades earned in new classes upon re-entry. Hallelujah!

This gave me a new beginning! I entered as a 1st year professional student, with three years to complete my degree. Credits transferred from Lee's College accounted for the first two years of the 5-year degree. Wow!

I became an **asking**, **discovering**, and **sharing** machine! I could not wait to learn more. I averaged 18-22 hours a semester for three years, even taking classes outside of the requirements of the professional degree. Little did I know that **asking**, **discovering**, and **sharing** were being branded in my brain. If our professors gave us a project, we darn well better have asked all the right questions regarding the decisions or **discoveries** we made when we presented our presentation to a jury of architectural faculty. Let me tell you that when our work was hung on the wall for review and comment, we had better have all of the proper answers to what was asked about our design, and why we made the decisions we did. We could never say, "I don't know." If we did, it was brutal! The professors were then all over us with questions. We had just opened the door for them to try and find out other things that we might not know, regarding our decisions. Sometimes they would say, "If your client asks you a question, are you going to say, "I don't know." Well, in reality, there are times that that could happen, but back then sometimes the students were like deer in the headlights when it came to answering questions. It was like going before a judge and jury combined, who were trying to find fault in what you had created.

If you survived, then your grades usually were good. Some of those juries caused students to drop out of the architectural program. But one thing is for sure, they stressed **asking** and **discovering**, and that also included looking. The architectural program trained us to look at things in ways that we never had before. Here is one example I remember in one of our drawing classes. The professor asked us to look at our forearm. He said, "Take your pencil and draw a one-inch square on your forearm. Then look at what you see, and make a drawing 24 inches by 24 inches, filling up the paper. Then show me what you see." That was a life-changing moment for me. I know I had to look very very closely at something that I had looked at before, but I never really saw the detail that was there before. After that exercise I never saw things the way that I had in the past. Everything I looked from that time on till today I examine closely. Quite often when we see things, we really don't see things, because we miss the little details. It's all the little details in life that comprise the wholeness of what we see, of what we do, and of what we believe. It even changed the way that I looked at writing.

"Beauty in now underfoot wherever we take the trouble to look. There are many panels fixed together, taller than they are wide. There is texture. Light is here, light is there, the scale is the same, but there is still change. I am very comfortable and very interested in all there is to see and hear and touch, like a child exploring an ever-changing land. Over and over again, I've found it impossible to memorize, but though, it always remains in the id. So much excitement I must explore!" H.I. Burns

The architecture program taught us to approach design freshly and with an open mind. But the professors did not want to see the normal in our work, they wanted to see the extraordinary! One problem that I remember vividly was that we were asked to take a cube and design a residential structure within that cube. I think I was the only one in my studio to turn the cube up on end.

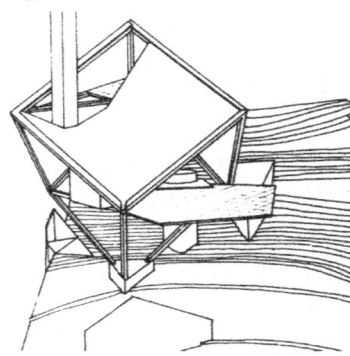

Sketch of my House Cube

My professors were surprised to see someone make such a bold move. I had a good defense, and I could answer all the questions which they asked about the decisions I had made to do this. To this day, I am grateful for my first studio professor, Sara Tate, who was such an inspirational teacher and guide.

The architectural education process became so mental that I even began to think and ask myself, "Well, what is our thought process like? What is the process we might go through while we are engaged in planning or deciding?" I even tried to illustrate the process. This is the first time ever that I have shown this diagram to anyone except for close friends.

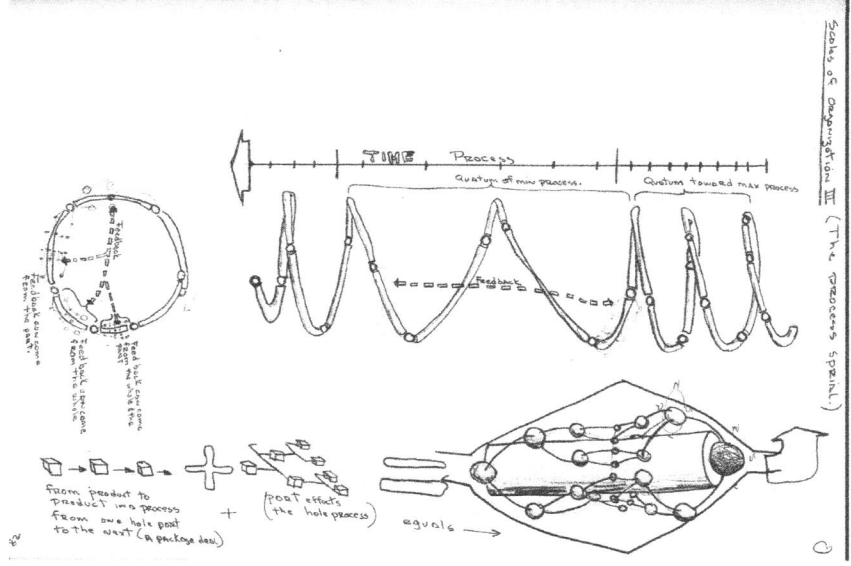

Image from the Sketchbook

At the top of the drawing, you see the decision spiral. Think of it as something akin to a slinky that can expand and contract. When contracted, a higher level of thoughts and decisions occur; **asking**, **discovering** and **sharing**. When the spiral is elongated, time also increases as to when action on decisions are reached.

In this process a thought could go in sequence like 1,2,3,4 etc., or a thought might have to be broken down or dissected into its multiple components and then reassembled through our mental filter, leading to action, or it could be both of these processes combined, taking us from one thought to another. Additionally, while this process is taking place, we might connect backward to other nodes in the spiral and other times, thus linking those results in combination with what is current in our asking and discovering process as we continue thinking.

As **asking**, **discovering**, and **sharing** continued, I became good friends with one of my classmates in the studio, Steve Rosa. I ran across an application from the Association of Collegiate Schools of Architecture, soliciting grant opportunities relating to architecture and education. Steve and I were first professional year architecture students then. I convinced Steve to team with me and apply. Together, we proposed that we would create a class that would combine architecture with education for the public schools. We called it Archology, a combination of architecture and ecology. In our class we would instruct teachers about how architecture could affect their instruction; also, how architecture could be introduced into the classroom, thus affecting social interaction. To our surprise, we were awarded the grant. Now we were ready to teach the class. But there was only one problem. We were freshman architecture students. How could we possibly teach a class to other students, particularly graduate students? We **asked** around, and we found a psychology professor who supported our efforts. He agreed to be the Quasi lead professor for the class, but Steve and I taught the class. You can imagine what your thoughts would be if you are a graduate student working on your master's degree in education and had signed up for class that was being taught by freshman architecture students. As it turned out, there were about 12 to 14 graduate students who signed up for our class. After the first day of class we told them about ourselves, and what our vision was for the class. They seemed excited, and no one dropped the class. It was amazing to see how God worked that out!

This is when I discovered another passion in life other that architecture. Obviously, it is tremendously rewarding to design a building and create a structure. But it is also tremendously rewarding to design a curriculum and to instruct others. Throughout the semester, we **shared** with our students how architecture could affect and effect a teaching environment. One of the graduate students who was teaching psychology at Henry Clay High School actually permitted us to come to her classroom and physically change the environment to observe the effects it had on learning with the students. So, we went into a typical classroom and changed the way students had to sit in that classroom, as well as the physical environment.

With the help of the students, we built a structure in a structure. The illustration shows the structure we made, which was a geodesic dome constructed of 380 yardsticks, 123 cans, and tinfoil. It took the students 2 days to assemble this structure. I think about 120 students participated. I am sure it was the buzz of the school at that time. It made the local news as well!

The Lexington Leader, Lexington, Ky., Monday, May 7, 1973 5

The School Set

Youth News And Opinions

Edited by Bette Pearce

NEW LOOK — Mrs. Angela Bullock's classroom at Henry Clay High School has taken on a new look. Instead of holding classes in a traditional desks-and-chairs setting, Mrs. Bullock and her psychology students meet under a large geodesic dome. The dome —designed by Herb Burns and Steve Rosa, third-year architecture students at the University of Kentucky, is constructed of 380 yardsticks, 123 cans and tin foil. About 120 students built the dome in two days. Mrs. Bullock said that the students constructed the dome to create a more relaxed atmosphere and to show that any space can be changed. (Staff Photo).

News Article About our Project

In addition to lectures, we gave mutiple slide presentations on extraordinary spaces in architecture to our graduate students on a weekly basis. We also created a way to demonstrate to elementary school students some concepts of architecture, neighborhood, and community.

I went to my wife's fourth grade classroom and others. Students were given a 6-inch square piece of cardboard. Next, each student was given a handful of wooden blocks of different shapes and sizes.

Student Project

Students were asked to make a neighborhood, keeping in mind that there also had to be streets and sidewalks.

We discovered quickly how creative they were, based on what we had asked them to do. After the students glued their block design to the cardboard, we asked groups of three or four students to take their 6-inch square neighborhood and connect it to one of their classmate's squares; the process was repeated until all of the squares would form a small city. It really drove home the concepts of neighborhood, community, and city for the fourth graders.

My three years as an architecture student were utterly amazing! Not only did I learn to **ask**, **discover**, and **share**, but I also learned about looking, seeing things, and listening, in ways that I had never done before. Listening and looking brought other opportunities as well.

Back in my second professional year as an architecture student, I **discovered** an amazing opportunity. It was a program called Vista Volunteer. If accepted into the program, I could work for a community-based organization for a semester, actually get architectural credit, and it would replace one of my design studios. There were three of us that applied for the program; Gary Violet, Dwayne Behne, and me. We went to work for an organization called The Housing Aid Corp. We had the privilege of trying to resolve housing issues with the underserved economical population in Lexington, Kentucky. We also could design community centers and show people how to winterize their homes to reduce their heating costs during the cold days of winter. On a larger scale, we were able to design a concept which was called a New Town in Town. There were many acres available from the old Odd Fellows' property, which became our site for a proposed new residential community. The organization applied for a grant through HUD. Unfortunately, we did not receive it. At this moment in my educational experience, I learned how to work with a community and tried to create a way to improve the quality of life through architecture. I guess we were a CDC, Community Design Center, before they were known as such.

Finally, that last semester of college arrived. The studio professor for our last term at UK was Vito Girone, who had studied at the École des Beaux-Arts. There were nine students in our graduating studio. That was a time of **asking**, **discovering**, and **sharing**, where I really learned the value of teamwork. For our final project we decided to work as a unit rather than working individually on our own projects. The project was a new campus center. We determined what each of our skills were, and what we each did best. We divided the responsibilities up to collaborate on a joint final solution. Some were better designers, some were better model makers, and some could render and illustrate better.

I discovered how **asking**, **discovering**, and **sharing** came together to help us achieve a common goal. We worked hard and long on this project. At one point, I remember working three days continuously, without any sleep. We were quite the studio! In our studio, strangely enough, we had a banana tree. Eventually, the tree grew a bunch of bananas. We were then referred to as "Vito's Bunch" because of the bunch of bananas that were on the tree. To this day, I am still in contact with some of my classmates.

Our Fifth year Architectural Studio at the
University of Kentucky

So, to all "Vito's Bunch", I want to say thank
you for **asking**, **sharing**, and **discovering** things with
me in our architectural studio. And thank you, my
classmates, and thank you, Professor Vito, for sharing
your knowledge with me. I think the picture shown
above was taken shortly after we took the bananas off
the tree, divided them up among ourselves, and ate
them. "Again, thanks guys. What a great Bunch you
were!" (Back row from left to right, me, then Joseph
Crouch, Steve Rosa, Gary Adams, Jeff Pearson, Front
row left, David Buschle, then Gary Violette, Ralph
Napletana, and Fred Merchant)

We finished up the year with a bang! I think

that our final presentation surprised everyone in its scale and level of detail, with all of the illustrated boards we did, and the model we created for the senior show. I personally think that we blew the other class studios away! That's just my opinion. We even printed a hard cover book of our senior project.

This previous college flunk-out did finally achieve his dream of becoming an architect, and in the process, was also inducted into the University's first architectural academic honor society, Tau Sigma Delta. It was a rough road for many. I think our attrition rate was somewhere between 70-80% from first professional year through the third professional year.

The work of architectural education was completed, and the door could now be opened which would lead to becoming a licensed architect, which I am still today.

Looking back now, what might I share with a young person as they contemplate what they want to do with their life? What should be **asked**, what should be **discovered**, what should be **shared**? These are the guiding principles that come to mind from my life experiences:

Here are some thoughts that I would like to share with you regarding ask, discover, and share:

Ask:
- Ask God for wisdom.
- Ask yourself if you are interested in a career because it's exciting. "Oh, I want to be a

fireman, or a policeman, or a doctor, or?"
Those are good career choices but make
them for the right reasons.
- Ask yourself, "Is this is what I want, or is this what others want for me?"
- Ask yourself, "Can I support myself and a family with this career?"
- Ask yourself, "Are there growth opportunities with this career?"

Discover:
- Discover what your talents are.
- Discover what you really don't like doing.
- Discover what steps are necessary for your career path.
- Discover if you can find a mentor to help and encourage you.
- Discover your real passion!

Share:
- Share with someone your ideas.
- Have others share with you about your dreams.

Keep in mind that your original pathway could change, but be sure that you make the absolute most of any determination you have decided on. Be prepared to make changes as they are needed. I am led to several verses in the Bible:

Proverbs 12 v11 "Whoever works his land will have plenty of bread, but he who follows worthless pursuits lacks sense."

Proverbs 18 v16 "A man's gift makes room for him and brings him before the great."

Proverbs 14 v23 "In all toil there is profit, but mere talk tends only to poverty." (Don't just talk the talk, but walk the talk, and achieve what you talk about.)

Graduation was now completed, and it was time to start looking for a real job. My wife already had a job as an elementary school teacher. She graduated two years ahead of me and was teaching elementary school in neighboring Bourbon County. During this time, she gave birth to our first son, Herbie. So now it was time for me to take the lead and be the major bread winner.

One of my professors, Sarah Tate, had designed a dental clinic in Goldsboro, North Carolina, that was fairly innovative in its design. In May, after graduation, one of my studio friends, Wade Dansby, and I decided to take a road trip to Goldsboro and see the project firsthand. On our way back to Lexington we drove through North Carolina, Tennessee, and into Kentucky. We stopped at between 72-80 architectural firms and academic institutions, looking for employment opportunities in architecture, and for me, in education as well. At this time, I either wanted to work with an architectural firm or find somewhere that I could teach architecture.

We did not have any leads, and the economy was terrible. I just had to fall back, **ask**, and **discover**. So, we **asked** where the architectural firms were, we found their locations, and made many cold calls trying to **discover** if there were any job opportunities. We left our resumes with everyone we talked with. The trip turned out to be very unsuccessful, as we never uncovered a single promising lead from anyone wanting to hire a recent architectural graduate. It was really a very discouraging trip. On a positive note, many of the people we did talk with said, "Please stay in touch, and check back in a month or so." Upon returning to Kentucky I compiled a thick notebook with brochures, pertinent information, and contact information, including a list of contacts from everyone that we spoke with.

In June, I went through the notebook, and I followed up on many of the leads that I had, with no results. In July, I went through the notebook again and followed up on the many leads that I had, with no results. In August, I did the same thing, however this time I had some information from an educational institution called Forsyth Technical Institute in Winston-Salem, North Carolina. I called on a whim to see if there were any open positions to teach architecture. They had just lost their senior instructor for the architectural program, and they said if my schedule permitted, I should come down the next Monday for an interview. Wow! I had an interview in one of my professional realms, architecture or education, and this was both. My wife and I left our son with her parents, and we drove down that weekend in preparation for my Monday interview.

When I arrived on the campus, I was greeted by the department chair of the engineering division, Walt Boggess, and he took me to meet the interview team for questioning. One thing that I remember distinctly about the interview is that I was **asked** if I could teach Statics and Strength of Materials. These would be courses involving engineering design. I told the team that I had never taught a courses like these before because it was more engineering than architecture, but if there were textbooks for these classes, I had good reading comprehension, and I didn't see any problems. I was **asked** many more questions and felt that I had done my research on Forsyth Tech and their architecture program. I answered all their questions in an exciting and eager manner. At the end of the interview they all thanked me for coming on such short notice and indicated there were a few other applicants they had to speak with. They stated that they would be back in touch with me. I returned to the hotel and shared with my wife that I did the best that I could. Now we'd have to wait and see what happens. The next day, we headed back to Lexington. The following Friday I got a call from the dean saying the job was mine if I still wanted it.

The pay was sufficient for me to support my family. With my wife's agreement and much prayer, I accepted the position. This was the beginning of August, thereabouts, and I had to be there ready to start before the end of August for the fall semester, 1975. We found a house to rent in our price range, we packed everything up in a U-Haul, and we moved our small family to Winston-Salem, North Carolina!

Now I began to make the shift from working on education in order to become an architect, to working at education and sharing my knowledge with others who wanted to **ask** questions and **discover** their talents about architecture and construction technologies. So, at 27 years of age, I began teaching professional architectural classes. Several of my students were many years older than me. I knew that if I was to gain their respect, I should never ever BS. If they **asked** me a question that I could not answer, my response was, "That's a really good question. I don't know the answer, but I will find out and let you know." I would always find out the answer to their question before my next class with them and **share** the importance of what they had **asked** with the entire class. This added value to the person that **asked** the question, and it allowed me to share a new **discovery** with other students, and learn, as well.

When you are at work, no matter what kind of job you have, there are always opportunities to **discover** new things about those you work with. One day I was teaching an architectural history class and made a comment about the students' work. What I saw the class producing didn't seem to have any energy, newness, or enthusiasm about it. It was as if they had never seen new and exciting things before, even though I was **sharing** some of those through history lectures. I said, "Let me **ask** you a question, and I want you to raise your hand. How many of you have traveled outside the state of North Carolina?" To my amazement, in a class of about 20 students, approximately 6 students had traveled outside the state. This was an utterly amazing to me! I **discovered** that the students needed an opportunity to see and experience exceptional architecture, wherever I could take them to achieve that.

It was in that moment that I **discovered** something must be done about this. I **asked** the students if they would like to have the opportunity to travel somewhere and see some architecture that was created by famous architects in America. The response was overwhelming. It was unanimous, and they were eager and ready to go. At that time, the only problem was that we didn't have travel funds. So, I created one of the early clubs at the college called the Architecture Club. We established fundraising events to raise money to help pay for our travel expenses, food, lodging, and gas so that we could go see some incredible architecture.

ARCHITECTURAL CLUB

Members: Back Row: M. Brown, W. Tucker, J. Strayhorn, G. Dudley, K. Carpenter, J. Dancy, J. Chandler, J. Bess **Middle Row:** J. Knopf, C. Jones, G. Foster, K. Smedley, M. McGee, H. Burns — Advisor **Seated:** D. Williams, J. Kendal, A. Sorensen, A. Robertson, B. Smisor, S. Walker

The Architectural Club of Forsyth Technical Institute was created to promote architectural education, to recognize outstanding academic achievement, and to provide related services to F.T.I. and the community.

This year's club consisted of 33 members who actively worked on fund raising projects for their annual architectural educational field trip to Chicago. Herb Burns served as advisor to the club.

Officers: H. Burns — Advisor, C. Jones — Sec/Treas., M. Brown — Pres., J. Knopf — V. Pres.

The first Architecture Club at Forsyth Tech

Our first trip was to Chicago, Illinois. For me, it was my second trip. My first was when I was in architecture school. Our club had yard sales, bake sales, cookouts, and car washes to raise funds. We finally raised enough money to take our first trip. It was going to be a long drive, so we took two vans full of students. We drove from Winston-Salem, North Carolina to Columbus, Indiana for our first overnight stop on the way to Chicago. I chose Columbus, Indiana because there was a company there called Cummins Diesel. That company would pay the architectural fee for any public works building, only if the architect that designed it was selected from the top 10 in the world.We got to see architecture designed by Eero Saarinen, Robert Venturi, Harry Weese, I. M. Pei, and Richard Meyer.

From there, we traveled to Chicago, Illinois. The students got to see all the amazing buildings in the downtown area. They saw where the offices of Louis Sullivan used to be, where the first skyscraper in America was built, and where the first elevator was built for a skyscraper. We rode up to the 110th floor of the Sears Building. We rode up to the 96th floor of the John Hancock Building to have dinner. We got to go to Water Tower Place and drive up and down Michigan Avenue, which is referred to as the "Magnificent Mile". We toured the University of Chicago campus. We saw the grounds where the world exhibition was held, and where electrical lighting was first introduced on a large scale. We went to the Chicago Cathedral. We toured Unity Temple, designed by Frank Lloyd Wright. We traveled out to Oak Park, Illinois and saw the studio of Frank Lloyd Wright, plus many houses that he had designed in the neighborhood.

That trip generated unbelievable experiences, with the students **sharing, asking** questions with each other, asking me questions, and **discovering** things in architecture that they had never imagined before. When we finally returned to Winston-Salem, I could see a freshness in their thinking. I could see a different look in their eyes when they began to attack a design problem, all because they had the opportunity to **discover**, firsthand, what others had done before. **We must never stop asking, discovering, and sharing!**

We all know that as we continue to work, everything changes around us in the world, including technology. When I was in college, I got a little bit of a technology bug in me. We had an opportunity to do some computer programming on a mainframe computer. Oddly enough, the programming language we used was called "Pagan". We could use this program to instruct the computer to print out a geometrical pattern based on the coding sequences we typed on a keyboard. It was punched out on a computer card. I was able to take a simple pattern I created, which then instructed the computer to rotate the pattern, multiply it, and offset it with particular X & Y coordinates. The result was a printed pattern from a single two-dimensional geometric form. As you know by now from what you previously read, **asking**, **discovering**, and **sharing** were embedded in my brain, and I could not stop continuing to **ask**, **discover**, and **share**. I **discovered** an opportunity to introduce computer graphics for the first time to my architecture students. It had not yet been introduced into the community college system in North Carolina. I convinced the administration to buy a Techtronic 4052. This was an early computer created before the days of personal computers. It had no internal memory, no math co-processor, and it had a small green screen with no color, except that of an oscilloscope green.

Forsyth Tech's first graphical computer

This is where the digital started at the college.

I think that occurred sometime between 1975 and 1976. The cost of the computer equipment was $10,000. The CAD class that I created was called Computer Graphics 151. This class was available, not only for architecture students, but for mechanical design curriculum students, as well. Lectures were given in the auditorium, as I had about 45 students in my class, but the computer was located in my office! The college was afraid that someone might break the glass on my door and steal the computer, so they took the glass out of my door, and they replaced it with a steel plate. Once a week, I would lecture the students in the auditorium about how to use this technology. When it was time for them to do their lab projects, they had to schedule a time to come to my office so they could work on this one and only computer, and complete their assignments, one student at a time.

Over the next ten years we continued to grow and expand our CAD technologies, moving from the one Techtronic to an Apple computer, then to a PC.

Finally, the math co-pressor was invented and changed the world of CAD technology. The company called AutoCAD created a software program that would allow you to draw lines and circles. We now could begin creating architectural plans on the computer and create construction documents. Soon, we had the first CAD lab in the state community college system. Others in our community shared what they had **discovered** about what was taking place at Forsyth Tech. Soon after, other regional universities inquired about what we were doing and **asked** me if I would be willing to help them do the same at their institutions. I was honored and privileged to create and teach the first CAD classes at the University of North Carolina at Greensboro, and then later, at Salem College in Winston-Salem.

Now, the interesting thing about work is that many people want to grow in their jobs, me included. At this time, technology was increasing at a faster pace than the college could afford to keep up with. I **asked** myself many times, "What can I do to stay mainstream with this early technology revolution? How can I keep hands-on with this evolution?" I was approached by one of my colleagues, Jim Kavitz, who was the head of the Electronics Technology Program at Forsyth Tech, to start a new computer CAD Cam consulting business with him. That was a serious change of work from what I was currently doing. I shared the offer with my wife about a career change, what it might mean, and the adjustments in our life that it might require, and I remember to this day what she said. Don't look back later in life, and say, "I wish I had done that." This was the encouragement I needed to take the leap of faith into a new work venture in my life. Always **share** with your spouse, if married, your visions and dreams, and **discover** together the strength and support that can come from that, even if that decision results in failure later. At least you were in unity regarding your direction.

JAKA was the name of the company that we started at that time, and I became V.P. of sales and training, and a minority stockholder in the company. For four years we were successful, expanding our offices into Virginia, becoming one of the nation's leading representatives for one of our CAD products lines, a software program called Versacad. We sold software, hardware, provided custom installations, and training. Our clientele included architects, interior designers, furniture companies, and manufacturing companies. We were very good at what we did. When we started, it was fairly easy to keep abreast of the newest and latest technologies. In a few short years, those technologies and new ones were emerging so rapidly that it became difficult to keep abreast and stay current with all the new technologies that were entering the marketplace. We **discovered** that when we entered this marketplace, we were the new specialists, and others had to ask us to help them incorporate these technologies. However, in just a short four years, some of what we were doing was becoming a commodity. Many more designers, architects, and manufacturers were discovering that they could purchase the software directly from the manufacturers and teach themselves, using the training tools provided by the software companies. Our company needed to make some adjustments to stay competitive, but we were not doing so.

At that same time, someone **shared** with me that the person who had replaced me at Forsyth Tech after I left, had just resigned. I did not leave my last job because I wasn't enjoying what I was doing. I just wanted to **discover** newer technologies in my field that I could not **discover** while teaching. I loved teaching, and missed it, so I called the V.P. at Forsyth Tech to see if they would be interested in me returning. The response was, "How soon can you submit your application?" I reapplied and stepped back into the position that I had left. There was a serious differential in pay compared to what I was earning at JAKA, but what was important was that they wanted me back, and I wanted to share all of the new technologies I had **discovered** with my new architectural students. I remained as a part time contractor with JAKA for several months. I loved JAKA and all the people I had worked with. God had reopened a door I had walked through once before, and now it was time to re-enter that door!

A lesson to share: Never burn your bridges because you never know when you may have to return to cross them again. Be professional in all you do in the workplace. Respect others, and become a contributor to what ever it is that you do. Become someone that employees will miss if you leave and not someone who will cause employees to be happy that you left.

For the next 27+ years at Forsyth Tech, because of **asking**, **discovering**, and **sharing**, I was involved in many incredible opportunities which included creating and starting up three new programs of studies; including Interior Design, Animation and Game Design, and Broadcast and Production Technologies. My **asking**, **discovering** and **sharing** also led to the creation of more than a dozen new curriculum courses, which were adopted by the State Community College System. Because of mission outreaches through my church, three international partnerships were created with colleges in Belarus and Ukraine, and I was able to take students on a couple of trips to Russia. Those are other stories for a later time.

Because of **asking** and being **asked**, the college assigned me the responsibility of being Coordinator of International Partnerships, in addition to my other responsibilities. I was honored to be one of the original collaborators in the creation of the North Carolina Community College Global Conference, NC3GC, a first in the history of community colleges in our state. The conference became a mechanism connecting other community colleges in an effort to **share** and **discover** international related activities.

I guess you have heard the expression, "Your education never stops." For me that is an axiom that stays with me even today. So, I enrolled at University of North Carolina Greensboro, UNCG, in pursuit of a MS degree in Interior Design. The title of my thesis was "The Evolution of a Solution". What? Yes, I was about to do some in-depth research to find answers as to how we create using current technologies; how we use those technical tools to carve out a solution to a given problem. There was a lot I **asked** my subjects to do. There were **discoveries** that I made as a result of what they did, and for the first time, outside of my thesis, I am going to **share** with you some astounding results that are being played out today, and with serious consequences.

I had a study group of six volunteers that were screened, in order to show that they had intermediate computer skills (basically they knew their way around the computer). The 6 volunteers came at 8:00 on a Saturday morning and were assigned to one of six identical computers with identical software installed. The volunteers were given identical problems to solve, and they had eight hours to complete the task. Little did they know that in an adjacent room, I had six additional computers set up in a manner that I could monitor, and see visually in real time, what each subject was doing every second. I took a screen shot every 30 seconds for their entire eight-hour test time. Later, I assembled the screen shots into six subject videos for review and analysis.

There were some amazing surprises during the evolution of their solutions. To the best of my knowledge, this is the first time ever that this type of research had been done back in 2000. The first **discovery** was that during the design process, while using CAD technology, none of the subjects had any recorded archive of changes that evolved in their design process.

Before the use of this technology, architects and interior designers frequently made sketches on tracing paper before committing to a final idea. All my subjects had sketch papers and pencils available to them during the experiment, but not one picked up a pencil to sketch anything! They elected to do everything on the computer, and the changes just evolved in the process. There was no archival history they could look back at and evaluate, to see if their current decisions were as valid as their previous ones. **A once highly practiced process was given way to the technology.** An alarm sounded in my head leading to a later thesis statement that **I should have shared much earlier.** My professors were encouraging me to publish the results of my findings, but I never did until now.

One **discovery** was that of the heartbeat or pulse in a design process, and were those design pulses similar? I looked at all of the digital executable tools the subjects could use, then looked at the time frame in which they were used and mapped an EKG or pulse for the solution.

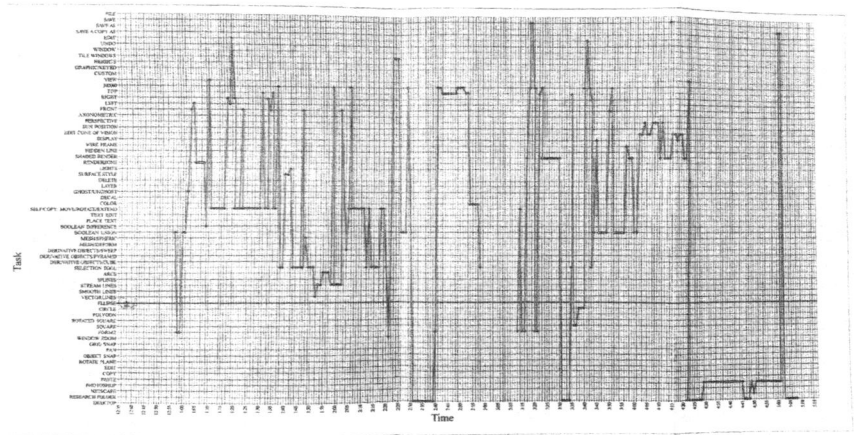

Illustration of a Design Pulse

This EKG for design reflected some similarities, but it also indicated individual variances as well. An important result was **discovered** from this research when using digital tools. It is vital to periodically record or archive at various stages in the process. It is important that you can look back and **discover** the previous design decisions you have made. It is important to review and consider the evolution of a solution as it moves forward. This must be taught as a part of the process in our educational pedagogy. Have trace evidence available to review at a later time, and this can be applied to anything you do in the work realm.

But what was the most **alarming discovery,** led me to propose the following hypothesis and theory, titled, **"The Evolutionary Technological Destructionist Theory".** Remember, this was back in 2000 when technology was beginning to explode. The theory, simply explained, means that the more technology evolves, the more destructive it can be to things we have historically learned how to do. For example, writing. How many of you write long hand now with a pen, pencil, and paper, or do you now type or say all your correspondence on the computer? Technology has destroyed or altered processes like this.

Concerning written language, I was never good at spelling. I have allowed technology to weaken my will to learn the correct spelling of words. How terrible! I just type now on the computer and rely on the technology to correct my spelling mistakes, which in effect, dumbs me down. Is this happening to you? We should use technology to our benefit, but are we destroying skills we have learned and used at home, and in the workplace? The technological tools now at our disposal, have eroded some of our skill sets.

I would always tell my students to work smarter, not harder, and that "time is money". I would encourage them to use technology to give them an edge on their competition. But I would also encourage them to control those technical tools and not to let those technical tools control them, or to control what their ultimate vision was.

No matter what technological tools we use, or what technology surrounds us, we must remain openminded, factual, and seek the truth, so that we can stay independent and make decisions freely, not following or accepting how all current technological tools might seek to control our thinking and doing.

This is important for my survival and yours as well. I have not found any articles discussing this prior to my thesis, but many more articles are appearing in the last few years. In reflection, I now see why my professors really wanted me to write about my findings and publish the information in a scientific journal. Now this has been shared with you, the reader, so be alert, and do not let technology control you or make decisions for you in the future. Napoleon Hill stated, "You are the master of your destiny."

As this chapter concludes, I have shared with you examples from my life experiences involving "Work" and my "Workless" efforts as well, in hopes that it might encourage you as you work on and in your life. The following figure reflects three basic concepts that I believe can lead to success in anything involving work.

As before, I am referring to a pyramidal-three-ring diagram with the heart at the center. Just as another reminder, all success, whether in the family, work, or in your faith walk, is controlled by your heart. You must have the right heart for success in whatever you do. I'm not talking about the medical heart but a heart that has the right love in it; for compassion, truth, and doing the correct things for yourself and others, and certainly not having a heart that could cause harm to yourself or others. So, if your heart is not right, you have time to begin giving love to others and put love into the things you cherish and do.

These three words, **leadership**, **results**, and

growth can interact with one another and do not have to happen in a specific order. Your leadership could achieve results, or growth could define the effectiveness of your results, and then your leadership. All three elements are totally interactive with one another.

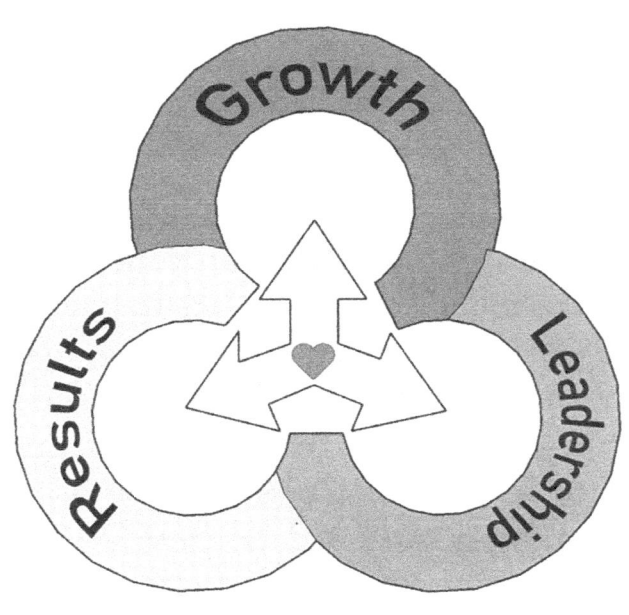

Rings for Success in the Work Environment

Let's look at each of these three words; **leadership**, **results**, and **growth**. In 2017, I gave a lecture to a group of business leaders in Lviv, Ukraine.

The title of the presentation was "Leadership in a Time of Crisis". Listed below are some of those skills required.

LEADERSHIP
Fearless Passion of Responsibility

You have to possess a passion and strength necessary to take on the role for change and success because you know that your leadership could cause change that some might like, and others might revolt against. But your fearlessness will help you to stay the course.

Calmness

In the wake of the storm you must remain calm. You cannot wear your feelings on your sleeve. Don't display your feelings openly, reacting to negative comments. Keep them private to maintain the calmness of those around you. A knee-jerk reaction generally ignites more harm and creates problems that may have to be smoothed out at a later time because you where not calm. Stay calm.

Vision

This is your foresight to see the future in a manner to take others where they have not been before. Be sure that you have thought carefully and clearly about where you want to go, and where you want your colleagues to go with you. Your vision must be grounded by past experiences and infused with ideas that will take you and your organization to a place of improvement, growth, and newness. This will become an example for others to follow. Remember, people of vision lead rather than follow. If your vision should fail, then fail quickly. Regroup, revive, and keep moving forward.

Leading by Example

If you lead by example, this means that you take responsibility for decisions. Good or bad, you are the leader. You have probably heard the expression, "Get your hands dirty." As a leader, you have to be willing to show that you can roll up your sleeves, do the same work that you expect of others, and show you are chipping in. Have a servant's heart! Do not expect your peers to do anything that you wouldn't do yourself. Respect is earned.

Communication

I will never forget a statement made to Paul Newman, who was the main character in the movie, "Cool Hand Luke". Luke had just been returned to camp after one of his escapes. The prison captain stated, "What we have here is a failure to communicate." I can recall many times in my career when communication was not clear, but intent was implied. You must be as clear as possible with all communications, as they will most definitely impact goals and results. I am sure you have also heard the expression, "Communication is a two-way street." You must also be a good listener, and be sure you clearly understand what is being communicated to you. If at anytime you are not clear, you need to ask that the information be **shared** again, at an appropriate time, so that you will discover the exact meaning of what is communicated. If you are **asking** someone to share with others your communication to them, be sure that they have sufficient information from you so that your message is totally succinct and understandable.

Self-awareness; Strengths/Weaknesses

When you look in a mirror, you see yourself, but you do not see how others see you. Several years ago, I had the privilege to attend the Center for Creative Leadership. (https://www.ccl.org/) This organization conducts research and evaluations of your leadership skills by evaluating your strengths and weaknesses. Prior to attending, those under your supervision complete a survey, identifying your strengths and weaknesses. Also, your supervisor completes a survey concerning your strengths and weaknesses. When you attend the leadership training, based on both the surveys and planned activities you engage in during the week, a final assessment is made, based on your leadership skills. Specifically, on the last day, your leadership advisor meets with you to discuss your strengths and weaknesses, then creates a plan of development for you that will strengthen your leadership skills. To my advisor's surprise and mine he said that he has never seen an evaluation like mine before. He could not identify any weaknesses and could not make any recommendations to me, except to continue to expand and develop my own leadership growth at whatever rate or direction I might choose. I am not trying to be boastful, because I know that I have leadership weaknesses, but I was shocked by his evaluation of my leadership, based on their evaluation techniques. He asked me, "What is most challenging thing for you in life right now?" I answered, "I am learning how to deal with and manage the recent unexpected death of my son. He was only 34 years old and died of a heart attack." His response was, "I offer my deep condolences."

My suggestion to you would be to ask those you supervise and those who supervise you for constructive comments or suggestions regarding your strengths and weaknesses. They may have suggestions for you to improve, or you might have to work on improvement on your own. We all want to be the best we can be, and that can only happen when we can capitalize on our strengths and manage our weaknesses.

Empathy

This is the heart connection in leadership, and it may be one of the more important skills. Everyone you work with feels connected more to you when you can **share** an understanding or feeling similar to what they are experiencing. Being empathetic is also letting someone know that you are there when they need you. Then they discover your willingness to help them through whatever they are currently dealing with. Empathy is putting yourself in someone's shoes or thinking about how they might like to be treated at work. Empathy can also build loyalty and create a stronger bond between yourself and others. Empathetic leadership can create a strengthened business loyalty.

But you must first understand your own feelings if you are to be empathic to others. Have you ever asked yourself, "What am I feeling?" When you do this, sometimes there might be rage. It is important to be quiet both externally and internally. Reconnect yourself to calmness, as mentioned previously. As someone once told me, "Think twice before speaking." Take in what you feel, digest your thoughts, and yes, reconsider your thoughts as you prepare to be empathetic with others. Above all, consider the consequences of your words and actions, and let them be for the right reasons.

Ephesians 4 v29 "Let no corrupting talk come out of your mouths, but only such as is good for building up, as fits the occasion, that it may give grace to those who hear."

1 Corinthians 12 v26 "If one member suffers, all suffer together; if one member is honored, all rejoice together."

1 Peter 3 v8 "Finally, all of you, have unity of mind, sympathy, brotherly love, a tender heart, and a humble mind."

Philippians 2 v3 "Do nothing from rivalry or conceit, but in humility count others more significant than yourselves."

Management Skills

What management skills are extremely important in leadership? Sometimes I chuckle at myself and imagine that I am a circus juggler, juggling 20-30 different objects at one time. At the busiest time in my academic career, I was at the same time:

- Teaching animation classes
- Serving as Program Coordinator for the Digital Effects and Animation and Game Design Programs
- Serving as Department Chair for Design Technologies, which included programs of study in Architecture, Interior Design, DEA, and Broadcast and Production Technologies.
- Serving as Interim Dean of Engineering Technologies, which included an additional 19 technical programs of study
- Serving as Coordinator of International Partnerships
- Serving on a variety of college committees

I was, to the best of my abilities, managing to help all areas grow and fulfill their visions. One might say that I was terribly busy and had a lot of leadership roles to fill. Many people asked me, "How in the world can you handle all of those responsibilities?" My response was, "good management skills." I rarely ever felt over-worked. I tried to give attention to everyone, I tried to communicate effectively, and I was always ready to help faculty and staff, champion whatever their own goals and objectives might have been for their particular curriculum areas, as well as those goals and mission objectives created by the president of the college and the board. I discovered that one must stay calm and organized to keep the cups from spilling over and the trains running on time (just an expression, as I think you know what I mean).

There is really no secret, other than to get organized. Since I had been teaching for many years, class preparation just involved some minor tweaking from time to time. There were three important tools I needed:

       1. A phone log
       2. A planning calendar
       3. a 'to do" notepad
       4. A journal (especially important)
       5. Email

The phone log I used allowed me to record important contact information and to make notes related to the tone and information of the conversation.

I tried to return missed calls as soon as I could, no later than the next day. That was my goal, anyway.

A planning calendar was a must. Because I was in the academic environment, my calendar did not run from January to January. It was an academic calendar which ran from August to August. This type of scheduling calendar was extremely useful.

Our staff and faculty service center at Forsyth Tech. had "To Do" paper note tablets, and they were so helpful! I could prioritize various goals and objectives in the order of execution. Did I always follow the order of execution I had laid out? No. But generally, I did. Some took longer than expected, so I worked on them, as I tackled quicker turn-around tasks. I suggested to those I supervised to take advantage of the "To Do" note tablets, and to use them to help manage their tasks and responsibilities.

Another vital tool that helped me manage was my journal. Everyone in management, in my opinion, must keep a journal. Being art minded, my journal was an 8x10 artist's sketchbook with blank pages. Every meeting I attended was journaled with the time and the date, what took place in the meeting, and what particular things required my action. Sometimes if the meeting was extremely long and did not connect with any responsibilities necessary for me to document, I would draw visionary sketches of sci-fi environments or unusual objects that would come to mind. But that journal was my connection to the flow of communication that occurred in meetings.

In trying to juggle everything, email was definitely the most time consuming. Many of my colleagues did not organize their mail very effectively. Their in-boxes were huge. You could scroll and scroll and scroll through hundreds, and in some cases, thousands of emails in their inbox. That would just drive me crazy! I created folders to archive all my emails by category that were important to save. While serving as the interim dean of engineering, it was unbelievable the number of emails that would come in every day. I really tried to stay on top of the flow.

One day I had finally recorded or responded to every email in the in-box, and it was empty. I was proud of that achievement and took a picture with my phone. One or two days later, while talking to one of the V.P.s, who at that time was complaining about all of the email he had needed to answer, I said, "Check out this image of my in-box," which was empty, and just by the look on this person's face I knew I should not have shown it. This is one of those times I should have thought twice before acting. So, my advice is to stay on top of all your emails, and manage them in a way that is most effective for you. But manage email, you must, or the email beast will consume you!

Integrity: Work Ethic/Professionalism

The definition of integrity is the quality of being honest and having strong moral principles, moral uprightness. "He is known to be a man of integrity."

What are some of the recognizable signs of integrity that are mostly demonstrated in leaders?

- Someone who is honest
- Someone who is sincere
- Someone who is fair
- Someone who works to help others
- Someone whose values influence others, promoting positive change

Wikipedia defines work ethic as "a belief that hard work and diligence have a moral benefit and an inherent ability, virtue, or value, to strengthen character and individual abilities. It is a set of values centered on importance of work and manifested by determination or desire to work hard."

During my career I always wanted others to think of me as a professional. There were things that I did that just seemed natural. Just looking like a professional in an educational environment goes a long way. As an instructor and administrator, I almost always wore a tie and was either wearing a sport coat or a suit. I did not want to blend in with my students and dress in their style of clothing. Many of my colleagues did not wear ties or suits. In fact, some wore shorts and t-shirts to class. I will admit that there are certain job functions in academia where a suit is not suitable, but not many. Even the choice of tie color plays a role.

1. Red: That's the power tie! Wearing it implies you mean business. It is a reaffirmation of strength and authority within the professional world. Whenever I was in meetings and wanted others to sense me as a leading player, I would wear the red tie.
2. Yellow: While still looking professional, the yellow tie conveys authority, intelligence, and positivity.
3. Blue or a dark color: It conveys trust, stability, and confidence. A blue tie is perfect for general public appearance or public speaking.
4. Other: When the only requirement is to look professional, wear a coat and tie. Sometimes the tie can draw attention to you because of the quirkiness or the patterns on the tie, worn only to be noticed in the group when you were not a part of the leadership in the group.

Sometime later, after I retired, I was talking with one of my students, and he said, "Mr. Burns, the students were really intimidated by you when they were freshmen." I was kind of shocked! I replied, "Tell me why you think that was." The student then went on to say, "They were coming into their first animation class as freshmen, and there you were! This big tall man in a suit, who looked so professional, serious, and authoritative." It's because I wanted them to realize that they were about to enter a professional work environment, and I wanted them to know who the leader was. The student continued to say that his classmates indicated that the majority of their instructors dressed like them, and they were not shocked. The student later payed me the highest compliment by saying that as they got to know me better, they really discovered how caring and concerned I was regarding their success as animators and how much I really loved them as students; that I would go out of my way to help them with anything, while still maintaining leadership and professionalism.

This reminds me of two other stories when I was teaching, involving integrity. I share these only that you might discover what impact your leadership could have on others. First, one of my former students called me one day to set up a meeting to discuss something. She had graduated about 10 years earlier. When I met with her, she asked for some advice concerning her desires regarding a potential change of employment. I was astounded and honored that she respected my thoughts and opinions and sought out my advice after ten years of her working in the profession. I guess my leadership had made an impact. The long and short of the discussion is that I told her to follow her passion, and indicated to her that she had the skills and confidence to become whatever she wanted, but if she failed at what she was trying to do, that would be ok. She would never have to look back later in life and say to herself "I wish I had only tried to do this years ago."

The second story is about another architecture student who had turned in a final project. Her project was the same quality of other "A" projects. I gave her a "B" on the project, and she became upset with me because she could see that her work was at the same general level of the others that received high marks. I told her that, yes, upon inspection this could be an "A" project. But I knew she could do much better than just matching the quality of others' work, and that I expected her to do her best in the future and not do work just for the grade. Well, at my retirement reception this student attended, and she shared with me that experience. Then she thanked me for encouraging her not to perform at the level of others, but to perform above that level, because I believed that she could! She said the experience was transformative for her and thanked me again for not accepting her second best, rather than her best. For me, that became one of the proudest moments for me as an educator. The act of **discovering** and **sharing** can motivate young leaders to realize their potential.

Attitude and Self-Confidence

I am sure that you have heard the expression, "Attitude is everything," "Your attitude is a decision," or as someone once said, "A bad attitude is like a flat tire. If you do not change it, you'll never go anywhere." Attitude is your foundation that can lead to self-confidence. Attitude has a lot to do with never giving up on your dream or passions. I had to have the right attitude and confidence that one day I would become an architect, and I succeeded!

You, too, can succeed with the right attitude and self-confidence. But what does it take? What can you do to build the correct attitude and self-confidence?

- **Celebrate wins!**
  Do you remember the feeling when you were victorious in a sporting event or class project, or with business success, and were able to repeat it? Your confidence in success grows.
- **Ask for help.**
  Asking for help will lead you to discover how to finish a task. It will build your knowledge base and increase your feeling of confidence and completeness. Also, it will strengthen your attitude for success.
- **Decide.**
  Have confidence to decide without having 100% certainty. Be comfortable in making your decisions without feeling threatened. If you have made a wrong decision, learn from it quickly, as you will soon be required to make another decision to keep actions moving in a positive direction.

- **Look confident.**
  Pay attention to your appearance, how
  you look, how you talk. Make eye contact
  when communicating. Maintain your smile.
  Have you ever been in a room, and someone
  walks in, heads turn to look at that person...
  putting aside ,someone who is dressed
  crazy or looks like a clown, but someone that
  is professional and looks like a leader and
  conveys a presence? I have been in places
  and observed this. It can be you when you
  have fully developed your confidence. But,
  a warning! You must not be egotistical. Have
  confidence, with humility, and your
  smile and demeanor will set you apart.
- **Help others to be successful.**
  Helping others become successful has been
  one of the greatest motivational building
  processes for me! As an academician, I have
  experienced no greater joy than when
  my students and graduates become
  successful. I know a great part of their success
  goes to them for their hard work, and their
  desire to be successful. But I know that I
  played an important part in their success by
  asking them to **discover** the New and **share**
  through their work what they have learned.
  You can view some of these successful student
  projects on this YouTube link:
  (https://wwwyoutube.com/user/FTDEA

videos). I love helping others be successful! So, if you have not started helping others, determine what you need to do, because that is part of what defines leadership.

RESULTS

We all know what results are. Can you remember some of these sayings? "For every action there is an equal and opposite reaction," or as my mother might say, "If you do that, you know what the results will be!" The Merriam-Webster Dictionary has this to say about results:

- to proceed or arise as a consequence, effect, or conclusion
- something that results as a consequence, issue, or conclusion
- something obtained by calculation or investigation

Results are most definitely consequences of actions. You may or may not have seen the term "ROWE" which means, "Results Only Work Environment". I cannot think of a job anywhere that results would be excluded from the work process. To be successful at anything in life it's usually based on results or achievements. Do you get a promotion for doing nothing? Usually, not. The promotion is based on your skills and experiences because of the results you have achieved through your work.

How can someone measure their results? First you have to determine what results you are

Mike Fishbein describes it best in his web post, "How Do You Measure Success or What I would Call Results?"

https://mnfishbein.com/how-do-you-measure-success/

- Discover your values.
- Compare yourself only to yourself.
- Measure what is hard to measure.
- Measure results over the long-term.
- Measure outcomes, not proxies.
- Learn and iterate.

Mike Fishbein's advice could not have been better stated.

"As you get older, your values will likely change. You will gain experience and learn what is most important to you. When I was younger, job titles and salaries were my metrics for success. Now, the way I measure success is far more robust."

Now I measure my success by:

1. What and who I put first
2. How I have helped someone else
3. Did I complete the goal or objective assigned to me?
4. My freedom to succeed at something not done before
5. Did I add to others, helping them ask, discover, and share, with desired results?

Do not be afraid to change how you measure success as you change as a person. These are lessons well learned for me, as well, when I reflect on past results in my life and plan for future results. I have shared my thoughts with you relating to results. Now let us look at growth.

GROWTH

Do you believe that any living thing or organization that does not grow, dies? Everything has a life or life cycle. A flower grows and blossoms, reveals its beauty and fragrance, and then it withers away. One of the certainties in our life is that one day we will die. Sometimes there is death in the work environment, and I do not mean a physical death, but the death of a business. If a business does not produce results that grow the business, it will die.

Everything grows and matures at a different rate. My academic growth was extremely slow in the beginning, but it accelerated as the right "fertilizer" was applied; something called motivation. When I talk with others who are not where they think they should be in life, I tell them that is ok, and that everyone's garden grows at a different rate and sometimes in a different season. But if they tend to their goals efficiently, their garden will also grow and produce meaningful results.

In a work environment, how do we purposefully effect growth in what we do? Sometimes in my History of Animation classes, I would share stories of the successful growth of others with my students as examples of excellence. Take Walt Disney! What an amazing story of a young man who had a vision, and how over time he grew that vision to become what it is today! He started in a garage. Or the story of Bill Gates, who dropped out of college and eventually founded Microsoft Corp. Or the story of Steve Jobs and Steve Wozniak, who out of a garage, eventually founded Apple. The long and short of my lesson to my students was to not let their age get in the way of their work growth. I would tell them again, as you have already read, that my grandfather told me "Can't never could do anything." You will never grow in work opportunities unless you **ask** yourself, "Can I **discover** what I need to do to start a business?" And when you do start that business, **share** the success to help that endeavor continue to grow. I would end by asking my students to think about where they would be five years from now, or ten years from now, and to think about what they would be doing. They had to develop a plan for growth.

If we want to grow in our work, what are some things to consider?

Write it down!

An important first step is to write it down! What should I consider? As an example, I am sharing with you some things I considered that could help me make sound growth decisions, as I was proposing to create many new programs of study and grow a design department, evolving into a design division.

First, start by asking some simple questions. Where are you now? Assess your current programs to determine if there are successful areas that stand out. Is the organization receiving adequate acknowledgement? Are the job opportunities adequate? Are you enrolled adequately to be viable in your business? Determine if you need to be lean. Are there underproducing areas? What do you need to do? Eliminate or enhance? Perhaps you need to close, and cut your losses, or perhaps you need to infuse with new equipment to become technologically current, or even update the training or the pedagogy of the process.

Next, record where you want the growth to go. As Interim Dean of Engineering, I asked the 73 faculty who led programs of study to develop 5-10 year plans for their programs and write them down. Some of the plans were only one page in length, and others were thirty pages. That's ok. Everyone developed their own personal plan of growth for the visions they had. I can honestly say that some of the engineering faculty had a variety of visions, but all had a vision of growth and wrote it down.

In order to grow you must discover your champions. Who is it in your organization that you, as a leader, can delegate leadership responsibilities to, at any level from executive to the workers? In some cases, especially in academics, but also in industry, are there champions in the community you can tap into?

- Are there current contributors?
- Are there current collaborators?
- Are there future contributors?
- Are there future collaborators?

When planning for growth, what resources do you have/need? Never forget that those in your organization can be resources, even those that you have not identified as your champions. Leave no stone unturned because of what you might **discover**. What equipment resources are there? Do you have enough equipment to handle growth? Is the workforce adequate to handle growth? Let's not forget the money. Is the budget adequate to accommodate growth? Writing your growth plan or vision helps you to see what ingredients are necessary to cook up that next great growth project. Write it down!
Then:
- Develop a timeline.
- Set goals and create a plan to achieve them.
- Understand the networking necessary or the tools required for growth.

Here is an excellent example of what was just explained. This example was prepared by Gisele Taylor-Wells, the Program Coordinator for the Interior Design Program. Gisele is now the Department Chair for Design Technologies, my former position at the college. Gisele is serving as a great leder. I hope this will provide a clear example when you create your own timeline for growth in your work. Although yours may be different, and I expect it will, perhaps this might give you a starting point.

Interior Design A30220

Timeline for Proposed Changes and Growth for 2017 – 2022
2017 – 2018
Start K & B Diploma Fall 2017 if cohort requirement is met
- *If the minimum is not met, we will need to assess the delivery format*
- *Options*
    - o *Alternate offering one of the K&B specific courses as an alternative summer elective?*
    - o *Offer online. This is a diploma geared toward those already in the profession or related fields to allow specialize in the K&B field.*

Expand our teaching space into 6200 when MET moved to the Carolina Building
    - o *Use that room for our non-computer-based introduction courses*

Expand the sample room / reference library to encompass all of 6201

Articulation Agreements:
- *Finalize the Articulation Agreement with UNCG's IARc program (SU 17)*

- *Further Discussions with NCCU's Apparel Design's Program (first contacted by them in SP 2017)*
- *Begin Discussions with Appalachian State's Program*

Resolution of needed faculty needs
- *Hire a second full time faculty member*
- *Maintain one adjunct to teach a class per fall and spring semesters to maintain variety in instructors for student's benefit*
  - *Commercial Studio*
  - *Professional Practices*

Incorporate more reflective writing into our program
- *More journaling*
- *Self-assessing of learning*

Continue to expand the number of Hybrid course offerings
- *Summer courses (DES 220, ARC 221, DES 238, and DES 275) were offered as Hybrids Summer 2017. Use these lessons learned to inform planning for 2017-2018*
- *Fall 17: DES 240 – Commercial I and DES 230 – Residential I will be offered as hybrid*
- *SP 18: DES 241 – Commercial II offered as a hybrid*

Update our Program Website

Increase the Program's Social Media Presence: Facebook and Linked In

One-Year Follow Up on Program Review Goals, 2013-2016 Review Cycle

2018-2019

Articulation Agreements:

- *Finalize the Articulation Agreement with Appalachian State's Program*
- *Reach out to other NC 4-year Design Programs: Western, ECU, High Point Univ*

Possible Relocation of the Program to OGC

- *SP 2017 – ID and Arch developed and presented possible relocation scenarios to the Dean's Council for the 1st or 2nd floor of OGC*

  Allocate and purchase needed materials for a permanent Critique and Lecture Space for ID and architecture.

New Plotter, if one has not already been purchased

Begin planning for a Statewide Curriculum Review meeting

Evaluate Student / Program involvement in competitions

- *Goal: have each student participate in two competitions during their 5 semesters in the program*

Evaluate the status of Hybrid courses

- *Current hybrid courses – successes / struggles*
- *Possible additional hybrid courses*

2019-2020

Re-evaluate the possibility of starting a Historic Preservation Program

- *Initiate meetings with Stakeholders*
- *Revise the proposed curriculum – update as needed,*

original drafted in 2015
Purchase new desks for main studio – preference would be to have a set up that allows for dual monitor set up.

Program Review for 2016 – 2019
- *Prepared / Update the Program Review Documentation*
- *Update Program Growth / Expansion Goals*

Curriculum Review / Update
- *Possibly initiate and /or host a Statewide curriculum review meeting/conference*

2020-2021
New Computers for the Main Lab, Current computers were purchase in Jan 2016 – this would keep with a 5-year replacement cycle.

Investigate offering one – two elective evening courses for students and industry professionals interested in specialized training: K & B focused courses, Digital Rendering, etc.

2021-2022
Review articulation agreements
- *Status*
- *Renewal or continuation as needed*

Technology and Equipment – in-depth review and evaluation

Begin outlining growth plans for next 5 years, reflect on previous 5 years

As you have read this timeline, you have noted that it conveys growth regarding facilities, faculty, funding, and re-evaluations to assess that growth is evolving as planned.

To **grow** in anything, you must have a plan, you must have **results**, and **leadership** must be in place to champion success. In the next chapter we will explore the most important role of all, and that is faith, which is the heart of everything.

CHAPTER FOUR

Faith

Beba, fe, geloof, glauben, Biba, wiara, hit, creideamh. No matter what language it is spoken in, the word "faith" is one of the most profound words in my life and the life of many others around the world.

Matthew 17 v20   "He said to them, 'Because of your little faith. For truly, I say to you, if you have faith like a grainof mustard seed, you will say to this mountain, Move from here to there,'and it will move, and nothing will be impossible for you.' "

As you have just read, faith can give you the strength to accomplish many things in your life. Faith in others gives you confidence in what others can do, and faith in our Savior Jesus Christ gives us eternal life and abundant life! What is faith like in your life? What does faith mean to you?

As a young boy living with my cousins, I had faith that my aunt would fix breakfast and dinner for us every day. She would make sure that we had clean clothes to wear. I guess those are things that we take for granted, but sometimes we take our faith for granted. As families, we all went to the same church every Sunday. As a matter of fact, the Burns and the Burklows filled up an entire church pew. Everyone at church knew that was our pew, not that we had our name on it or anything, but you know how it is; everyone knows where everyone sits in church. I had faith that every Sunday after church my mother and I would stop by Balls Ice Cream and buy an ice cream cone to eat as we headed for home. My favorite was butterscotch ripple and black walnut. That's not really the kind of faith that can change our lives or lives of others. How do we consider faith sometimes?

•I have faith that everything will be ok.
•I have faith that you can...
•I have faith that they will figure out what to do.
•I have faith that I can do this.
•I will be yours, faithfully.

Why is it important to have faith? As you and I know, things do not always go as planned! I screwed up in college and had put myself in a terrible situation. That can be a cause for one to lose hope and lose faith. It's easy for us to say to others in those situations, "Just pull yourself together," or "Pull yourself up by your bootstraps." If you do say that to someone, be prepared to offer them some faith direction, too. Be prepared to share some of your knowledge and experiences with them that involve your faith.

Your faith in the workplace often is displayed without your knowledge, as others are watching your life. Your attitude says a lot about you, your conversations say a lot about you, your practices say a lot about you. People see you in ways you never think about. Faith can light you up like a beacon that might draw others to you, and when that happens, you can encourage, enrich, educate, and enlighten someone. That will start a spark of faith in them, perhaps.

I was once in a former Soviet country. I was surely a stranger in a strange land, hearing a strange language. Walking down the street, I observed many people not looking at each other. Many had their heads bowed with unhappy looks on their faces, while I was walking upright looking around at everyone and everything with a happy expression. Well! Someone eventually asked me, "Why are you always smiling?" Remember when I advised you earlier to think twice before you speak once. This was not one of those times. My instant response was, "My love for God is always with me." I guess that's why I seemed so cheerful and content. I guess they saw a faith in me that I was not aware of. You never know when God is going to put someone in your path for a purposeful reason. Always be prepared for that. Never leave your faith at home when you go out.

Faith is purposeful and can give you courage. There are some scriptures that capture for me the meanings of faith and courage.

Luke 12 v25 "Who of you by worrying can add a single hour to your life?"

Psalm 23 v4 "Even though I walk through the darkest valley, I will fear no evil, for You are with me; Your rod and Your staff, they comfort me."

Deuteronomy 31 v6 "Be strong and courageous. Do not be afraid or terrified because of them, for the Lord your God goes with you; He will never leave you nor forsake you."

Psalm 27 v1 "The Lord is my light and my salvation— whom shall, I fear? The Lord is the stronghold of my life—of whom shall I be afraid?"

I pray these words will increase your faith in difficult times. There are other times in my life, as well, that faith has given me courage and strength and peace. I was laying on a gurney in a hospital getting ready to be wheeled away for triple heart by-pass surgery. My wife said to me, "You seem so calm. Is everything ok?" My response was, "Sure. I am either coming home or going Home." Her response was, "I want you to come home!" My point is that faith can give you peace in times which could prove to be extremely serious in your life. Just think of the many Christians that have given their life just because of their faith. Now that's real courage! Could I/we do that?

I just briefly touched on faith in the work environment, but what about faith in your family? Why does it seem that in today's times, many parents are not sharing their Christian faith and values with their children? I know there are many that are, but what is happening in those other families? I observe that many parents say they are Christians, but they do not take their children to church to be exposed to others of faith, or to learn those important faith values. What can we do as parents?

- Spend time with our children talking about Jesus and faith.
- Share scriptures at home.
- As a parent, we can learn from our children. There are times that we can discover from our children. Be ready for those times to listen and learn!
- We can pray with our children. Not only at bedtime, but at meals, during the day, and also to provide help in crisis situations. I still remember times that my mother prayed with me. Hopefully, your children will have similar memories.

- Certainly, we should tell our children what we believe because we are the example for them in the family.
- We might be surprised some day to discover that our children have been asked by their friends, and they shared our family faith values with them.

Remember that with faith comes wisdom, grace, and trust, all which will reinforce a perspective of faith. Be sure that the foundation you build is solid, and that you will always be there to protect it.

Have faith that God has a purpose for you. Looking back on my life, I can recall at least five times that I could have lost my life! There were also times that I was a failure in business. You already know about the time that I failed miserably in college. There have been other things that I have failed at in life. It was because of faith that I never gave up. It was through faith that I discovered what my potential is, and that God has a plan for me. So, be still in your faith, and listen. But there are also times to rejoice in your faith. Let me share with you some images and thoughts from my recent book, "Route 66 Have You Found Your Route in Life?" The book is my illustrated journey through the Bible, asking, "What does this mean?" Then, discovering those meanings for me and sharing my experiences, so others might connect with God, Jesus, and the Bible.

The first illustration I created shows King David rejoicing.

2nd Samuel 22 v1 "And David spake unto the Lord the words of this song in the day that the Lord had delivered him out of the hand of all his enemies, and out of the hand of Saul."

King David Singing Praise

The faith application and tasks are that anyone can fail, even if they are blessed by GOD, just as King David was. We must protect our minds and hearts, so as not to wander. We must remain humble, not prideful, and resist the temptation of ungodly thoughts and actions. Isn't it much better to do the right things in life, rather than to constantly ask forgiveness for our sins and wrongful actions?

Let me challenge you to look heavenward, outstretch your arms, and sing praise to God for your blessings and His forgiveness for your sins. Ask God to show you what you can do for Him. Then be still, listen, and look for His signs in the future for you.

The second illustration is from Book #62, I John. John writes this letter to churches in the region of Ephesus about 90 A.D., to churches he had probably ministered to in his earlier missions and church plantings. It is suggested that these writings came from Patmos while he was in exile there. John talks about the light and darkness in faith. 1 John 1 v4-7 "And these things write we unto you, that your joy may be full. This then is the message which we have heard of Him, and declare unto you, that God is Light, and in Him is no darkness at all. If we say that we have fellowship with Him, and walk in darkness, we lie, and do not live by the truth: but if we walk in the light, as he is in the light, we have fellowship one with another, and the blood of Jesus Christ his Son cleanseth us from all sin."

John talks about right versus wrong, light versus darkness, and love of God versus love of the world. John also speaks about love in action.

I John 3 v18 "My little children, let us not love in word, neither in tongue; but in deed, and in truth."

From the Dark to the Light

Application:

What a perfect book for now, considering all the discord around us in today's world! It seems that some people are persecuted just for not agreeing with the position of another person, especially about a political position or a view about life itself. There is truly light and darkness in our times, there is truly good and evil in our times. The choice is ours to be the seeds of light, the seeds of love, the seeds of truth, the seeds of faith, and the seeds of action in the name of God and Jesus Christ. We can be available to help those move from darkness into the Light.

My challenge to you is to be a godly example. I hope the illustration will reinforce visually the sacrifice Christ made for us because of His love for us, and that as Christians, we have a responsibility and should have a willingness to lead others out of darkness into the loving Light and principles of Jesus Christ, as a result of our faith. Will you be a leader for Christ? There are many people that need you!

Have you noticed that a heart is at the center of the illustrations for family, work, and faith, with the words love and faith being most important?

None of what I have previously written about can succeed, be bound together, or influence other parts, without being at the center of our **asking**, **discovering** and **sharing**. The real motivation in our hearts should be the love and faith we have. It's the engine that drives our success, lifts us up from our failures, carries us into the future, then upward into heaven. **Is your heart right?**

At the Heart of Everything.

CHAPTER FIVE

Experiences of Others

This chapter is near and dear to my heart. My route in life has engaged me with others that have had amazing life-changing moments. I have invited these very special people to share with you an extraordinary time in their lives and to contemplate one event in their life that involved **asking**, **discovering**, or **sharing**; that totally altered their life and way of thinking, and that involved their family, their work or their faith. It is an honor to share their stories with you, the reader. What follows are amazing testimonies that I pray will give you encouragement, guidance, and vision in your life regarding **asking**, **discovering**, and **sharing**.

Last Minute Decision
by Gary Griffith

Dwight was a teenager when the great depression began. He lived on a farm and times were tough. In his late teens he was able to get a temporary job working for the township, breaking rock to pay back taxes on the family farm. It was tough work and the township made employees break a predetermined distance of rock every day. People who were not able to break the required amount of rock were fired. Dwight was a kind man. An example of this was when he helped another employee who was not able to break his quota of rock.

Dwight worked hard on the family farm, was a good money manager, and eventually got a farm of his own. He regularly put in 70-hour work weeks. He was a respected member of the community and was successful enough to have the Pennsylvania Potato Growers recognize him and feature him in their magazine. Dwight didn't devote much time to activities not related to farming and didn't have much time for "organized religion". As a child he was baptized and went to church with his parents, but as he got older, he drifted away without knowing what the Gospel Message meant. He had a rift with the church when, although he had not attended church for years, the church still had him on their membership role. A couple of volunteers tried to strong arm him into pledging for a building project by stating they would post on the church bulletin board the amount each member pledged. Dwight ordered them off his property and was "burned up" at the church for years.

Dwight had a son and daughter. He was a kind and generous father and dearly loved his wife. He patiently taught his son farming, work ethics, and money management. Some of his son's fondest memories are working on the farm and being taught by his father.

Eventually age and ill health took Dwight's wife, and made Dwight unable to live alone. He lived with his daughter for a while, and then with his son. His son was a believer, and over the years, attempted to witness to Dwight a couple of times, but was rebuffed with bitterness and anger.

When Dwight went to live with his son and family, his health was extremely poor. His son's wife bought Dwight a large print Bible, and the son and his wife highlighted the Roman Road with a marker, and then outlined it on tablet paper because they felt Dwight would have trouble locating the verses.

Dwight's son and his wife **discovered** Dwight's Bible would be moved nearly every day. During this time, the son again explained salvation. One evening the son asked Dwight the question, "If you were to die tonight would you go to heaven?" The question was met with hostility, and the answer was, "This is for only God to decide." Meanwhile, the Bible continued to be moved daily. A few weeks later the son asked the same question about dying. Dwight's response was, "What kind of a question is that? Of course, I know." The son's response was, "How do you know?" and the answer was, "Because I have God's Word. It is His promise to me." As he exclaimed this, Dwight poked his twisted arthritic finger into his Bible! Rejoice, an answer to years of prayer, and to the work of the Holy Spirit!

A few weeks later a blood vessel burst in Dwight's brain and he went to join the Lord. Because his son, Gary, **shared** the Word with his father, Dwight, in a loving way, his dad was able to **ask** himself where he was in his faith, and then he **discovered** the pathway to his Heavenly Father.

About - Gary Griffith

1964-1966 Allegheny Technical Institute, Pittsburgh Pa.

1966-1999 Employed by AT&T at various locations in Pennsylvania, White Plains New York, and Virginia. Career included technical positions and managerial functions in engineering departments.

2000-2002 Employed as a contractor in a Top-Secret function for the Federal Government.

2003-2006 Senior Engineer for Qwest Communications overseeing telecommunications at various U S Embassy locations in Europe and Asia.

2007 Retired, now living in Winston Salem

Least Expected
by Henry Williamson

One of the most powerful and life transforming things I learned was from my son, Clay. He was in college and visited us up at the lake one weekend. He and I were out on the pier fishing late one afternoon and I decided to ask him this question, "If your dad were to die tonight, what one thing would immediately come to your mind about him?"

His answer was totally unexpected! He said, "Do you remember when you put the wrong kind of dishwashing liquid in the dishwasher here at the lake, and it sprayed suds all over the kitchen?" I thought to myself, "This is the most memorable impact I've had on my son?" Then Clay explained, "You didn't have a fit of rage or curse or scream at anyone. You assumed responsibility, just cleaned up the mess, and put the correct kind of dishwashing liquid in the dishwasher. That really taught me something about handling problems and crisis situations."

What Henry **asked** his son led to the **discovery** at that moment when he **shared** this: You don't have your most influence and impact on those you care about WHEN YOU PLAN IT, BUT IT HAPPENS SPONTANEOUSLY, WHEN YOU LEAST EXPECT IT. IT'S USUALLY DURING A CRISIS MOMENT!

That important lesson has stuck with me during the rest of my career and life, especially as it relates to leadership impact.

About – Henry G. Williamson Jr.

Former Chief Operating Officer (COO) of BB & T Corporation in Winston-Salem North Carolina, USA. BB&T is the nation's eighth largest bank holding company with over $250 billion in assets. During his career, he was commercial (business) lender, a commercial loan administrator, an Area Executive with responsibility for a number of banking offices, and later became part of the company's executive management team with responsibilities for human resources, financial operations, information technology, banking operations, legal, audit, and the banks fee-based businesses.

In 1989, he was named the Chief Operating Officer, until his retirement in 2004. He obtained his undergraduate degree in business and his MBA from East Carolina University. He currently serves as director on the board of Hooker Furniture Corporation, a manufacturer and exporter of wood and upholstered furniture, where he serves as Lead Director. He has a wife Nancy, two adult children, and five grandchildren.

A Man in Another Land
Charles Morrison
by Herb Burns

When Charles graduated from high school in 1954, he did not have a clear path of what he wanted to do in the future. But he did know that he didn't want to stay home and work on his family farm. Several of his friends where entering military service, and Charles took some time to investigate other services and to ask his friends about their choices. After a review of the possibilities, it seemed that the Coast Guard would be the best, considering all of the options, and in fact, he just liked the Coast Guard.

Charles enlisted, and he began to **discover** what he was able to do in service to help his officers and others. So, Charles became a petty officer in the Coast Guard! He learned discipline, respect, leadership, responsibility, duty, and many more life skills that would prepare him for future events. He served 4 years in the Coast Guard and upon leaving, he had saved enough money to begin his college education.

Charles entered Campbell College in North Carolina, which was a two-year institute at the time. Not clearly knowing what he was to major in, he was informed that he had to have at least two years of a foreign language. His choices were German or Spanish. He decided on Spanish and took the other classes necessary for graduation. While he was attending Campbell College, another year was added to their program (now a three-year degree).

Charles **discovered** that his Coast Guard experiences had provided him the life skills necessary to manage his time, goals, and educational responsibilities. Charles was also older than many of his academic colleagues, and his previous life experiences had prepared him for academic success. Upon graduation, he again had to **ask** himself "What am I going to do now?". Someone had **shared** with him that they were considering going to work in the Peace Corps. So, he looked into it and applied, met all of their requirements, and was assigned to the town of Cumana' in the country of Venezuela. Having taken two years of Spanish gave him a definite advantage.

Charles was surely a man in another land, as he was placed in the role he was expected to fulfill. His assignment was to teach English and coach athletics at Antonio Jose' De Sucre High School there. Charles was now in a place where **asking, discovering,** and **sharing** was essential to his surviving and impacting the lives of those at the school where he was working. Charles was on his own! On a personal note, I speak a little Russian, and I've been in countries where I have had friends to help with me with the language, getting around town, and meeting others. I can imagine what it would be like to be alone and to get around on your own. Charles' courage must have been incredible; to be immersed in a foreign land for the first time in his life, to teach high school for the first time in a foreign country, non the less, to coach athletics for the first time, and to discover a new way of life for the first time when the native language was not his own.

When I asked Charles to describe what the school was like where he worked, he said that it was surrounded by big fence with barbed wire on the top. When the students came in the morning, they would lock the gates, and no one could come or go until school was over without special authority. Charles said that the students wore uniforms to school much like a parochial school in America. When I **asked** him about the fence with the barbed wire on the top, my question was "Who are they trying to keep out?" Charles' response was they were trying to keep out the rough Communists. Wow! What a **discovery** that was for me.

At this time in Charles' life, since he was not totally fluent in Spanish, **sharing** became a two-way street for him and his students. If he did not know the Spanish word for something, he would simply just point to something, and the students would tell him what it was in Spanish. Sometimes, he would even make a gesture, and they would explain to him in Spanish what the gesture meant. Funny as it may seem, some of the students were speaking in words to each other that he had not heard before in Spanish, and when he questioned them, they were actually cursing at one another. So, Charles made himself a little notebook of all the foul language so that he would be able to recognize when the dialogue among the students was not as it should be.

Charles also coached basketball at the high school. He **discovered** quickly what Spanish basketball was all about. You would grab the ball, run as fast as you could to the other end, and then you would make a layup. The students did not understand team play or passing the ball! Charles was from the country where basketball was invented, the U.S.A. He taught them team discipline, instructed them through basic drills, and they **discovered** what a team playing together was all about. In talking with Charles, I discovered that he was extraordinarily successful as a coach. Venezuela was having a National High School basketball tournament, and his team was selected from their state to participate. He told me that his high school team finished third in the nation. So, not only was he leading the students in the classroom, but he was also leading them outside the classroom as a coach, a personal mentor, and a true friend. He was someone that they could trust and go to for advice. He was truly a great representation of what American men and Christians should be.

There was only one church in their town, and everyone attended it; the Catholic Cathedral. Charles was from America, and many of the students had questions about the Christian faith. Charles was a member of a Baptist church, and they were not quite sure what that was all about. So, Charles, to the best of his abilities, explained to them what non-Catholic Christianity involved. I **asked** Charles if he felt he had any impact on those that he talked to, and he expressed concern that he had lost contact with some of his former students. But I am sure knowing what I have observed about Charles over the years of our friendship, that he made a tremendous impact on many lives in Venezuela in the town where he taught school.

I am certain that Charles' work there really exemplifies what **asking**, **discovering**, and **sharing** is all about. Those three words created the bond between him and his students. This later prepared him in life for tough and challenging times.

Charles' experiences and his willingness to share with me will hopefully be an inspiration to others who find themselves at a place in their life where they need the strength where **asking**, **discovering**, and **sharing** can make a lasting impact. "Thanks, Charles, for sharing this part of your life with me and the readers."

About – Charles Morrison

1956-60 United States Coast Guard as a Petty Officer

1960-63   Graduated Campbell College with a degree in Social Studies

1963-65   Served in the Peace Corps, teaching English and as a sports coach in Cumana', Venezuela.

1966 NC Certification teaching HS Spanish

1967-1992 Taught Spanish for 25 years and retired from Reynolds High School in Winston-Salem working for the WSFC School System

Finding a Friend
by Jack Bales

Feeling alone, really alone is not a good thing. I can remember two grades in school (the 6th and 8th grades) when I felt alone, that is, friendless. Oh, I had schoolmates around, but felt ostracized for reasons I fail to understand even to this day. Maybe because I was not a standout in sports or not particularly smart or handsome, or whatever, it was a difficult time.

Time passed. I was in my freshman year in Bible college. One day after my last class for the day, I happened to be walking by a table in the school lounge/snack bar area. There sat a man who I judged to be about 35 to 40 years old (I found out later he was 39). He was in a discussion with some other students about a biblical issue that sounded interesting to me, so I sat down to listen. After the discussion was over the other students left, and it was just him and me. We did not know one another, so we began talking small talk to get acquainted. I soon **discovered** that he, too, was a freshman and had decided to begin college much later in life that most folks. I also **discovered** that he had gone through a bitter divorce. This struck a chord with me as a similar thing had happened to me. He was very surprised that someone as young as me (I was 20 years old) had gone through such a thing, too.

We soon ended the conversation, and we went our separate ways. The next day, to my surprise, after the class day was over, he found the rooming house I was living in and came to visit me. We had a long conversation about life, being a Christian, the Bible, and so on. As the days went by, we became closer and closer friends. To help us both with expenses, he **asked** me to be his roommate, and we split the rent and food 50/50. After classes each day, we would spend hours sharing and talking theology. For the first time in many years, I had a close friend. I considered him my best friend, even though there was 19 years difference in our ages. To this day, I consider him the best friend I ever had.

After the semester was over, I ran out of money and decided to go live with my parents for a while and go to work with the goal of saving money and going back to school. One day, to my surprise, he showed up at my parents' home looking for me. He told me that he, too, wanted to work, save some money and had no ties in Nashville, Tenn. where we had met, and that he considered me his best friend. Thus, he got an apartment, and we continued the friendship and the long talks about God and the Bible. I looked at this as a kind of Paul and Timothy relationship. I can't tell you how much I grew spiritually during those days. He also joined the church where I was a member, and we teamed up as a pretty decent team of evangelists who made an impact on that church.

In a few years, a couple of wonderful ladies came into our lives and we both remarried, not at the same time, but within about a year or so of each other. Our new families became very close, and we would remain close friends until he and his wife passed away. I now have been married to my wife for 45 years. As I look back on it, I can't tell you how much it meant to me in my walk with God for an older saint to take me under his wing and nurture me through a very difficult and lonely time. No other person in my life has had such a positive influence as did Eldon Wade Trimble because we **asked**, **discovered**, and **shared** together important parts of our education, expenses, and life experiences. Thanks again, Eldon, for being a part of the transformation in my life!

About - Jack Bales

Jack came to Christ at the age of 11. At 16, he felt called to go into some kind of Christian Ministry. As a result of this, he was given the opportunity to preach at various churches & youth meetings around the state of Florida where he was living at the time. After graduating high school, he worked for a few years at various jobs to earn money to go to college. Jack chose Free Will Baptist Bible College (now Welch College) to do his undergraduate studies, while also taking classes at Belmont University and Fort Wayne Bible College. Jack graduated in 1978 with a B.S. degree, having majored in Bible & Elementary Education. For the next 37 years, he would work in the Insurance Industry in various roles in the Underwriting, Marketing, Sales & Claim departments, all the while, being involved with the ministry of teaching, and sometimes filling in for vacationing pastors.

In the early 2000's, after a series of revival meetings, Jack felt led to begin graduate studies at Trinity Theological Seminary, concentrating in Christian Apologetics. Jack finished his studies in June of 2011.

From 1975 until now, Jack began building a theological library which now consists of almost 1000 volumes. Jack completed a book entitled "Thy Kingdom Come" in 2002, which remains unpublished. He currently is rewriting some chapters and hopes to publish it soon. His hobbies are fishing, camping, target shooting, flying model airplanes & performing magic (Illusion) shows. Jack has been married to America Bales for 45 years. Jack now teaches a Sunday School Class, and Bible Study at Calvary Baptist Church, and is a host of a popular podcast series, "Three Men for Thee" https://3-mft.fireside.fm/ He and his wife Meky have one daughter and one grandson.

In the Seminary
by Slavik Pyzh

What makes seminary effective is that seminary is much more than getting information or giving away information, it's about forming values and attitudes. Our vision is very simple – we want every local church to grow through baptisms and discipleship. We are convinced that mentorship is the way for changes to take place. Mentorship relationship between a program director, mentors, and their students, will help each student become more effective in what he/she is doing in the church.

Principles of Mentoring

1. **Ask** yourself, "Can I become a servant to my students?"

Christ demonstrated that principle. He emptied himself for others and He humbled himself to help others so that others would become different. The mentor doesn't take freedom from his disciple, he doesn't restrict him, he doesn't take away resources; instead he always **asks** himself, "What I can do to help?" The mentor gives away his experience and knowledge, and he gives away himself. There is no room here for fear, but there is always a reminder that we are here together.

168

2. **Discover** your success by achievements of your disciple.

Christ didn't measure his personal success by his personal achievements, but instead, by achievements of his disciples. The mentor thinks of himself as a servant to his disciple. The mentor lives and acts only for one purpose. That purpose is for his disciple to live according to his full potential. The mentor doesn't seek for his personal achievements, but he rejoices in the achievements of his disciple.

3. **Sharing** and mentoring helps his disciple to carry the burden for his mistakes.

Christ lived and served and gave His life as a ransom for many. Christ took our sins and our mistakes on Himself. The true mentor understands that he is accountable not only for the successes of his disciple, but also for his failures. The mentor doesn't have a right to say "Look, I told you…" Instead mentor says, "Your mistake is my mistake, your burden is my burden." The mentor is the one who gives away vs takes away. He desires your success and not his personal achievement. He's willing to carry the burden for mistakes of his disciple and not to look for someone to blame. The mentor is the person who walks by your side for the rest of your life.

About - Slavik Pyzh

President of Ukrainian Baptist Theological Seminary and National Coordinator for The Global Leadership Summit in Ukraine, undergraduate degree from SW Seminary, earned his Ph.D. from Southwestern Baptist Theological Seminary in Systematic Theology for his dissertation on Baptists in the Soviet Union.

Twice Broken, Then a Champion
J. C. Martin
by Herb Burns

I have known J. C. and his wife Barbara for many years, as they were members of our Bible Fellowship class at Calvary Baptist Church in Winston-Salem, N.C. We have personally heard many stories about their life and experiences while J.C. was a professional baseball player. I recently asked him if he would consider sharing with me some life changing experiences involving **asking**, **discovering**, and **sharing** that he had along the way to becoming a World Series Champion baseball player with the New York Mets.

After having dinner with J. C. and Barbara, J.C. began his story. He was born 1936 in Axton, Virginia. His father was a deputy sheriff of the county, and J.C. proudly displays his dad's badge and sheriff patches, framed and on display, in his study, along with many of his major league pictures. His family life included a strong Christian faith. Church was required every Sunday, and as much as J. C. loved to play baseball, his father would not permit him to play on Sunday. At that time, J.C. felt baseball was more important, but he respected his father's wishes, which also included no smoking or drinking.

In high school J.C. was an outstanding baseball player and was scouted by the White Sox. After graduation, J.C. went to Chicago to try out. He ended up signing for $4,000 with the White Sox Triple A team as a first baseman. While in the Chicago area, he met Barbara, his wife, and there are other great stories to be told about Barbara and J.C. Those are stories for another time. As life continued with baseball, one day one of his teammates was loosening up in the batter's box on a road trip. He accidently hit J.C. in the mouth with a lead bat and cracked his front teeth. His mouth got infected, one of his eyes was swollen shut, a real problem, but he had to play through his injuries.

When he returned home, his wife thought she was ready to deliver! He got ready to take her to the hospital, but the abscessed tooth burst. J.C. fainted several times and had to be cared for by a neighbor. Finally, he got Barbara to the hospital, but it was not yet time for her to deliver. Baseball, being what it was at the time, prompted him to leave for another road trip with the team, still with an abscess. He had to leave his wife back home. In those days of baseball, the teams did not have extra players, and if one was absent, they could not field a team. It was difficult leaving his wife, and there were no means of communication, no cell phones back then, which added to the physical and mental conditions he had to manage. And just think about his wife, Barbara!

When the team returned home to the clubhouse after a 10-day road trip, J.C. discovered that the manager had J.C.'s bags packed. He shared with J.C. that another player from the majors was being sent to the team, who was also a first baseman, and that J.C. would be sent down to the D League because this new player would replace him. J.C. was heartbroken! A successful player in the A League with the aspiration of moving to the majors was now being sent down to a lower level to play. At this point in his career, J.C. was just ready to quit. Was all of this worth it?

When he arrived home, he **asked** his wife, "What are we going to do? I am ready to give this all up!" While they were there sitting in the living room, Barbara reached over and picked up the Bible on the coffee table and Read Psalm 121:

"I lift up my eyes to the hills-- where does my help come from? My help comes from the LORD, the Maker of heaven and earth. indeed, He who watches over Israel will neither slumber nor sleep. The sun will not harm you by day, nor the moon by night."

They bowed their heads and prayed. They concluded that he needed to continue. "Let's go on," was the quote. J.C. was broken for the first time and realized that he needed to lean on

Christ. It was life changing, and from that time on he depended on the Lord. Life with baseball eventually took a turn, and he finally made it to the Majors. On September 10, 1959, at Comiskey Park, Martin started his first major-league game as a catcher with the White Socks. J.C. had a great career with the White Socks. They finished second to the Yankees in the Pennant Race, just a few games from making it to the World Series.

There are other stories in J.C.'s life. There was a time when his son had swallowed some medication inadvertently and was turning blue, not breathing, and with no hospital nearby. So J.C. turned his son over, and with the top of his hand, started slapping him on his back. Eventually, he started breathing again and returned to normal. Then there was the time during spring training when they were warming up and running around the field, that J.C. could not keep up with the other players. He just didn't feel good because his side was aching. He went into the club house, and the trainer said it was probably gas. He told him to put the vibrator on his side to break up the gas. J.C. held it there until it was too hot for him to hold. He went home still with an aching side. At home, one of the neighbors was a nurse and came over to see if she could be of any help. She asked J.C. to pull his leg up towards his chest. Then she pulled it straight away from him. J.C. screamed in pain, and the nurse said to go directly to the hospital. There, the diagnosis was that he had appendicitis. His appendix was removed, and the doctor said that if he had waited any longer that it could have burst, and he might have died. In both cases J.C. said, "God had a hand on us at every turn." Little did he know that he was about to be tested again.

Later that year, after having a great season with the White Socks, and almost making it to the World Series, he got the dreaded news again. "You are being traded to the N.Y. Mets! "What? I am being traded from a 2nd place team to a last place team!" He felt like he had been broken again. But his faith was stronger now than before. So, while he was with the Mets in 1967, playing as their catcher, the team won the World Series! J.C. was broken twice, found the Lord, and became a World Champion! J.C. had to **ask** himself why these things were happening, and along the way he **discovered** how to put his faith and trust in the Lord. He is now **sharing** this amazing journey with you. Eventually, he returned home when he was traded to the Chicago Cubs on an Easter Sunday morning.

About – J.C. Martin

1959 Signed with the White Socks
1967 Traded to the N.Y. Mets
1969 World Series Champions (w/N.Y. Mets)
1970 Returned to Chicago to play with the
       Chicago Cubs
1972 Final season in baseball
1975 Martin worked alongside the legendary
       Harry Caray on WSNS-TV for the White
       Sox.

J.C. Martin spent 13-14 years playing in the big leagues, seeing the best players ever; guys like Bob Gibson, Willie Mays, Carl Yastrzemski, Al Kaline, Willie Horton. J.C. also was the catcher for five Hall-of-Fame pitchers: Wynn, Wilhelm, Seaver, Nolan Ryan, and Ferguson Jenkins.

A Deep Look Into Mom's Heart
by Steve Whitley

There were very few days in my adult life that I did not phone my mom before I hit the doors of BB&T, the bank for which I worked. Prior to the days of cell phones, it was the last thing I did before hustling out the door. When cell phones became the norm, it was a conversation I had on my 12-minute drive to work.

The purpose of the call was for two reasons – the first being to check on her, and the second simply to hear her voice. It was a soothing voice to me, a loving voice, an encouraging voice.

My mom became a widow at the age of 40. I was 17, in college, a younger brother and sister at home with her, and I just liked to check in. She liked it too. There were many pressures with no husband to turn to, her oldest son learning the ropes of college life, and the deep loss she felt losing the soulmate she loved so much.

Even on her "not so good" days, there was a positive, caring, supportive tone in her voice. I felt so special because she never seemed hurried or distracted. It was as if her world stopped for the 2 to 4 minutes we talked. I **asked** her how she was doing, did she need anything, and really listened to see if I could **discover** that anything was bothering her. I usually **shared** what my day included, and any news that might interest her.

Prior to ending the call, she never failed to tell me how special I was, how much she loved me, and that she would be praying for me that morning.

These calls went on for years. As time passed, they became even more relevant, meaningful, and such an integral part of my day. I would share my schedule for the week with her on Monday. She wrote down the critical things, strategic meetings, trips involving air travel, or troubling personnel issues. Throughout the week, she would ask how a particular meeting went, and if I had to fly, she knew the departure and arrival times. I can hear her saying right now, "Steve, don't you be anxious about anything. I have bathed you with prayer this morning. God will be looking after you." She always insisted that I call her when I landed, and I always kept my promise to do so.

The last 15 years or so, the short calls got richer and even more meaningful. The spiritual component became more of a centerpiece as she would share scriptures and prompt me to do my part in Bible reading, prayer, and quiet times to just listen for His Voice.

I asked Mom one day how she was able to be so "on top" of everything and add such spiritual depth to our calls. What she told me has shaped my life to this day. It was a discipline she had discovered and adopted that had, according to her, "revolutionized" the time she spent with "her Lord," as she would say.

Mom shared that in the book of Matthew, chapter 6, verses 5/6, she had learned that she needed a "secret" place to pray and read scripture, and that she had turned her closet into that place. She said that the time she spent in there had grown from 10 minutes to one hour, minimum, when she was **sharing** this with me.

In her calm, humble, yet powerful voice, she shared what it meant to turn off the world of television, cars going by, kids playing and screaming, and turning on God's world, a world of quietness, deep thought, and meditation. When I asked her more about the discipline, she shared that 5:00 am was her start time and that 6:00 am was her end time every day, without exception. When I **asked** her why so early, and how did she make herself get out of the bed, she reminded me that I work out that early, almost every day, and why that priority could possibly be more important than hers! I listened, I learned, and I stopped talking! This was serious business.

Well, as months and years went by, my morning calls went as follows: "Good morning Mom, how is your day going?" Straight to her "closet" time she would go. "Let me tell you what I learned in Leviticus this morning." 'Leviticus, Mom?" I might say. "Now, how is Lynn's cold? – better, I hope." "I believe your flight is at 10:30, right? How did that meeting go yesterday?" How would anyone not yearn for these supportive words.

Then, as always, she would say, "Just know that I have bathed you in prayer today, Son. I will continue to pray for you. Please know how much I love you. Please call me when you get there."

I do not know how many planes stayed in the air and didn't crash, or how many meetings went well, or how many blunders I avoided because of the prayers of my Mom. All I knew, and was reminded of each day, is that she was praying, starting at 5:00 am, and continuing throughout the day. My brother and sister and others were included in that hour as well. I do not know how they were affected either, but what a feeling knowing that you know someone is constantly praying for you.

About 6 weeks before my mom passed away, Lynn and I were staying with her. We stayed there most of the weeks prior to her death. She needed our support and our care, and we gave both willingly, as we had received so much from her. One night I asked mom if I could walk into her special closet. I walked in, looked at her tattered and torn Bible, gazed at this place where she taped special notes to the wall, so as not to forget them. I saw my name up there and tears filled my eyes. I saw various devotionals she would use to enhance her spiritual journey.

Something caught my eye, and I went out and asked mom about it. I said mom, what is that stool doing in there? It doesn't have a back on it and looks so uncomfortable. Where is your chair?

She looked at me so seriously, and said, "Steve, there is no chair. I do not want to be so comfortable when I go in there. I want to be alert, praying, listening, sometimes pleading when I spend time with God. I have got lots of spiritual work to be done in there. Comfort just hinders me."

Well, Mom is at her eternal home now. I was honored to share the last 4 hours of her life with her. I sat by her bed which was located directly across from her closet. I stared at it as I rubbed her hand. I told her so many times that night what her prayers had meant to me and others, and how much I loved her. I saw the end coming, and I promised to her that her legacy of love and spiritual devotion would never die.

The finality of her last breaths was chilling to me. Her 92 years on earth had ended. I couldn't believe it then. It is hard to believe it now.

As we were cleaning out her house weeks later, my siblings and I were discussing important things that each of us wanted to keep. I had already selected a shirt that she wore frequently, and reminded of her. The only other thing I desired to keep was the stool from the closet. It symbolized the attributes of her heart and the yearnings of her soul. I do not want the memory of those to fade.

The stool sits in a small upstairs room that Lynn and I call our "nest." We read and watch television in that room almost every night. I glance at the stool often. It brings me peace. It brings me joy. A smile always comes to my face. I feel her love.

No one will ever know how many times I have picked up my cell phone early in the morning to call Mom, and just before dialing, I am jolted with reality. You see, for a millisecond, she was going to take the call. Her soothing voice was going to answer.

What a legacy she left to so many. How many generations, in big and small ways, will be touched by the days she spent in that secret place? How many chapters in God's providential plan of life did she write? How many souls have, and will be saved by her cries for His mercy and grace?

About – Steve Whitley

- Born in Albemarle, N.C. in 1947
- Moved to Richmond, Va., In 1989, and then to current residence in Lewisville, N.C. in 1998
- Currently Retired after a 40-year career in banking, the last 20 years at BB&T in Winston-Salem serving as manager of sales

- Married 46 years to Lynn Whitley – 3 children, Leslie, Allison, and Cameron – Blessed with 7 grandchildren ranging in age from 8-23
- Have been a church going, salt and light servant of Christ since the age of 32 – prior to that filled a pew on Sundays, but not a lot of evidence of the faith
- Teaching and openly sharing the precious Word of God is a passion – an honor – and a duty I feel God asks of me
- Member of Center Grove Baptist Church, currently serving as Life Group Leader
- Likes are working out (physical fitness), enjoying time with my family, especially the precious retired freedom to really connect and spend time with Lynn, and teaming with her to watch acceptable television and movies, (hard to find!)

Seeing Faith through a Friend
By Linwood Lewis

In mid-2002, I received a call from the president of our company informing me that an employee in our Winston-Salem organization was just diagnosed with cancer, and the prognosis was not good. The president knew that the company could support the employee with medical and material benefits, but he **asked** me to walk along side of him from a spiritual perspective. All my managerial training was useless in this situation, except that it was widely known that I was a believer and gave God the credit for the successes both in life and in business.

For the last twelve months of his life, the employee, Victor Clark, and I **shared** a journey of faith and accountability that greatly strengthened both of us. Victor was already a believer, and the lay pastor in an African American church in Winston-Salem. It was never "Why me, Lord?" but "What are you trying to teach me, Lord?" in all of our prayers. I **discovered** at the end of his earthly journey, and it was very evident to me, that Victor had taught me much more than I had imparted to him. Victor showed me how to die a death that glorified God.

When God calls you to do something outside of your comfort zone, always revert to the truth of God's Word and the peace that passes all understanding. Always be an effective witness before your employees at work, as Victor's Home-Going was a tremendous testimony to every employee in our business. Like Esther in the Old Testament, you may be "called for such a time as this."

About – Linwood Lewis

A United States Navy veteran during the Vietnam War era, Linwood held senior executive positions within the General Electric Company and B/E Aerospace (now Collins Aerospace). From the beginning of his career, he felt a calling from God to treat the business world as his personal mission field. During those years, God granted Linwood access to numerous business executives around the world, allowing him the opportunity to instill in them a legacy of success and significance. Today, he continues to bloom where he is planted through mentoring, teaching, personal security, and Board of Deacons' service opportunities within his home church in Winston Salem, NC. Linwood and his wife, Laura, have been married for 46 years, have two adult children, and one grandchild.

God Shows Up in the Midst of Turmoil...
by Kenny Patrick

After working 21 years for IBM in Boca Raton Florida, I accepted a buy-out offer and left the company.

In 1998 I moved back to Lexington, Kentucky to open a business for my sister. We started a small school on Walton Avenue. We developed and wrote short courses to train people who did not want to go to college or could not qualify. Once a student successfully completed the course, we issued a certificate of completion and assisted the student in finding employment. We offered computer utilization and nurse aid training to begin the school. Our intention was to offer more practical training, and our list was long. Within one year we certified over 200 people who all passed the state nurse aid exam, and all had jobs in the field in less than a month after passing the exam.

I was convinced that I had **discovered** exactly what God wanted me to do. After all, we were helping struggling people make their lives better. The school was growing quickly and appeared to be on the right track.

My sister had a partner in Canada who invested her money, several million dollars, along with 1 million dollars of my retirement money. He would transfer money to my sister when she requested. This money was used to support the school while getting the business on its feet.

The day came when he stopped communicating with my sister. She soon discovered he had embezzled all our funds. Try as she did, through Canada's legal system, she was never able to locate him, or recover the money.

Along with my niece, my wife, and I used personal money to pay the instructors and ensure the remaining students could complete their courses. As so many others have experienced...I now felt abandoned by God....

It was in the midst of all this turmoil, I experienced an encounter that I will not forget.

A day after learning about the possibility that all our funds were gone, I left my office, and drove up Walton Avenue to Woodland park. An empty bench caught my eye, so I walked over and sat down. Feeling depressed, alone, even a bit scared, I sat there **asking** "God, why? Where are YOU?"

A short amount of time passed when I noticed a man searching through a garbage can. He was looking for food. As he was unwrapping pieces of paper, I got up, walked over, and put my arm around him. I **asked** him to come sit with me. I immediately reached into my pocket and took out all the money I had and handed it to him. "You can get yourself something good to eat," I said. We sat there and just talked and shared for a while. I had to get back to work.

As I was about to get up, he reached over and patted my hand. He said, "God will bless you for helping me. Thank you."

As I walked back towards the sidewalk, another thought came to me. I will go get him some more money. I turned around...looked toward the bench, and he was gone! I walked around the park trying to locate him. He was nowhere to be found. I turned toward the bench as I was about to leave. There was a single bright light shining on the bench where he had been sitting. It was then I **discovered** God was testing me to see how I would react while I was on the bottom. Would I keep my focus on myself, or would I **discover** that I need to get back to His business of helping someone in need? After that experience, I made the decision to watch, every day, for someone who needed help, physically or emotionally, then, act accordingly. This godly experience gave me the vision to write the following poem which I would like to share with you

A Walk in the Park
by Kenny Patrick
Richmond, Kentucky

I walked through the park and I saw him.
He was worn. He was torn. He was sad.
I could tell he was cold and was hungry.
I reached down to see what I had.

I was sure he was homeless and lonely.
I debated with me what to do.
As I looked even closer, I noticed
on his feet, there was only one shoe.

Watched him limp to the can full of garbage.
Then, he searched to find something to eat.
I no longer could watch without acting,
so, I quickly jumped up on my feet.

I approached and put one arm around him,
as I told him how sorry I was
that life somehow hurt him so badly.
He replied, "That is just how it is."

I decided to give him some money
and gave him whatever I had.
We sat back on the bench and kept talking.
He smiled and no longer seemed sad.

He told me he knew God would bless me.
We shook hands and I went on my way.
I turned back to the bench where I left him.
I remember that sight to this day.

For you see he no longer was sitting.
I could find him nowhere in the park.
All I saw was a bright light still shining
on that bench when all else had turned dark.

About - Ken Patrick

I am retired and still wish to make a difference in this world. Having written and published several small books, it is my desire to share them. My hope is that the reader is inspired, encouraged and prompted to think about himself/herself and take actions toward self-improvement. A key result I have in mind is to stimulate your thoughts and cause you to act and encourage others. May you decide to love others in such a way that you will change lives that otherwise would never change.

My greatest encouragement comes from my wife, Carol Patrick. She received her Doctorate in Educational Leadership from the University of Kentucky and is a professor at Eastern Kentucky University where she teaches Child and Family Studies. Music has always been a part of Carol's life experiences. This site also includes inspirational songs performed by Carol and some friends with whom she sang over the years.

If you would like to read more of Ken's poetry and inspirational writings, visit his web site below:
https://theresalwayshope.webs.com/

The Grape Gatherers
by Jerry Pegram

The year 2003 was a terrible year for my wife, Avalene, and me. Avalene had lost her job eight years prior, due to a relocation of headquarters going overseas, and now my job was eliminated because of a buyout. For the first time in my working career, I was unemployed. At 61-years old, with no family income, I was terrified. I remember praying for a job. Also, our Bible Fellowship Class was praying, but I still had no job. I remember **asking** God, "Why?", and then I remembered scripture that teaches us that trials in life bring us closer to Him.

Twenty-two years prior to this, I had established a small one-acre vineyard at my home. During this time, along with five other men, we had founded a very small winery, called Germanton Vineyard & Winery, located in Germanton, N.C. This was never a money-making venture, but more like a serious hobby. However, my small vineyard at my home did provide me with enough income to pay for property taxes, house, and car insurance.

In mid-August, I developed a cough which I thought I could treat with over-the counter medication. By late August as I became worse, I finally agreed to go to the doctor. I was diagnosed with pneumonia and told to stay in bed at least two weeks or my "next stop" would be the hospital. That got my attention. I was so sick that my granddaughter, Madison, asked her mother if I was going to die.

During this time, the grapes were ripening beautifully. It was truly a vintage year, but also a year in which the grapes would rot on the vine because of my confinement to bed. One night a friend in my Bible Fellowship Class, Ken Pruitt, called to check on me. During the conversation, he **asked** about the grape crop. I told him the grapes were ready to pick, but I did not have the strength or the help to harvest, and that this year would be a total loss. He **asked** if I would mind if he made a few phone calls. I wasn't sure exactly what he was up to, but I said, "Sure." He called back a little while later and said he had pickers lined up, and "When do we pick?" The following Saturday, nineteen cars with people from my Bible Fellowship Class showed up to pick grapes. I later **discovered** that Ken had cut short calling class members due to such an overwhelming response. Some people were even upset because they were not called, but Ken very wisely knew that too many pickers in the vineyard would be difficult to manage. The 35-40 people (half of our class), picked three and a half tons of grapes in three hours. My father, my son-in-law, Mark Long, and a friend, John Glass, were trying their best to keep the pickers supplied with boxes in which to put the grapes. I remember my father saying, "These people can really pick grapes!" Dad grew up during the depression and was used to hard work. What he saw that day in the vineyard made a lasting impression on him.

During the picking Avalene was in the vineyard taking pictures. She came back to the house to give me a progress report, and she was in tears. **I asked** her what was wrong; and she said, "I just can't believe what is happening, and what these people are doing for us."

When the pickers were finished, they rolled up the bird netting, picked up empty drink bottles, and came back to the house to see me. When I went out to thank them, I was very weak, pale, and had lost a lot of weight. I will never forget the look of concern and love in the faces of these Christian friends. I had never in my life experienced or seen this kind of sharing love outside of family.

Throughout the New Testament, Christ teaches us to love one another. Never was this sort of love more visible than on that hot August day in a small vineyard a long time ago.

As I write this, sixteen years have gone by; and it seems like yesterday. The financial crisis has long passed, my health is good, even for a 77-year old, and God has blessed me abundantly. I no longer depend on the vineyard for income nor do I make wine for the winery. The small vineyard is still producing grapes, and I enjoy

sharing the fruit of my labor with friends, some of whom took part in this special harvest of love. Today, I am still in awe at how God took such a terrible personal experience and turned it into a blessing that I will never forget. I will always consider this little vineyard as "God's Little Acre".

Lessons Learned

Today as I look back, I honestly believe that my illness was brought on by worry. Christ tells us, "Do not worry about tomorrow." Matthew 6:24.

During this time, I was regular in attendance at church, involved in a ministry in my Bible Fellowship Class, and even ushered. All of these things do not create a strong faith. God knew this and wanted me to depend on Him for "all" things.

My prayer life was not as strong as I had thought. A strong prayer life requires a strong faith, obedience to God, persistent and fervent prayer.

I **discovered** that this experience made me more sensitive to the hardships of others. Remember, our trials won't last forever. **Ask** God what He is trying to show you.

About - Jerry Pegram

Born in Winston-Salem, North Carolina in 1942. Graduated from R. J. Reynolds High School in 1960. Went to work for R. J. Reynolds Tobacco Company after graduation. Joined the U.S. Navy January 30, 1964. Served aboard the USS Saint Paul (cruiser) and aboard the USS Kitty Hawk (carrier) off the coast of Viet Nam. Returned home (honorable discharge) October 1966. Joined R. J. Reynolds Tobacco Research shortly after returning home. Joined Schlitz Brewing Company in 1969. During the 1970's , was one of the founders of the award-winning Germanton Vineyard & Winery and helped form the Piedmont Grape Growers Association. But more blessed than all of the awards is my marriage to my wife, Avalene. I am now retired and enjoying Bible study, the vineyard, friends (who I share wine with), my daughter, Christy, her husband, Mark, and my three grandchildren.

God is Enough
by Jan Killmeier

"And we know that all things work together for good to those who love God, to those who are the called according to His purpose." Romans 8:28

"Faithful is He who calls you, who also will do it." I Thessalonians. 5:24

"He who began a good work in you will perform it until the day of Jesus Christ." Philippians 1:6

I am not who I was, but who was I? I was who I thought I was, and who others thought I was, but was that who I really was? Who am I now? Is this the real me? And where did and does God fit in my life? Was God enough? Was He with me? Living His life through me? Did He guide me to where I was? What understanding of God and His Word did I have then? What do I have now? Who am I?

I knew I had made a huge mistake when on the drive from Pensacola, Florida to Pittsburgh, he's driving 80 miles an hour on a two-lane road around the Smoky Mts – laughing at my asking him to slow down. The last thing my mother said to me at the wedding was, "I am moving to GA. where teachers are paid year around; you cannot come back home."

We respond to the level of emotional and spiritual maturity that we have at the time. Having gone for counseling in 1974, I discovered that emotionally, my growth was truncated at age 10 when due to many incidents, I gave up on receiving love and security – consequently, I've experienced a life filled with insecurity, thus anxiety. Unfortunately, when the mind cannot cope with reality, the body suffers. Therefore, throughout my marriage I suffered from digestive problems; the good part was that my weight stayed around 120 pounds.

My mother, sister, and I moved a lot during my growing-up years. (7 different schools in 12 yrs.) In spring, 1950, we moved to Talladega, AL, where I was saved at Vacation Bible School three months before my sixth birthday. I loved the new church family. Becoming a child of God definitely changed me, even at a young age. I learned that Jesus loved me, died for my sins, and I was forgiven and felt so relieved! So, every time the doors were open, we were in church. My best memories are from memorizing scripture in childhood VBS's. Scripture memorization was a big deal back then. Everywhere we moved, I walked to the neighboring churches' VBS programs every summer and loved it! (At one, I won my first Bible, which my husband later cut up for verse inserts into his sermons.)

Although knowing God made a huge difference in my life, survival itself was a challenge. My parents had divorced when I was 2 ½ and my sister was 4. Coming from a "divorced home", we were looked down upon in 1950s America, and were considered less than acceptable by society in general. We rarely saw our dad after that. My sister Dianne, all her life, was looking for our dad to come home and love her, so she tried four marriages, then killed herself in 1982 at age 39, leaving three teenagers (one of whom killed herself at age 28). I was a survivor, and since Dianne's 4th husband had joined her, I was the one cleaning out the condo and making funeral arrangements.

My mother was a teacher and a school principal, so her time and life were 98% dedicated to "bringing home the bacon". My sister and I were just there. But in defense of my godly mother, her mother had died when she was a baby, so her 12-year-old sister raised the other 6 kids by her dad, who never remarried. My mother, toddling around looking for a mother, was passed around among siblings who resented her, so they either ignored her or spoiled her while their dad worked out in the fields all day. So, she never grew up emotionally. She did not know HOW to mother, and since she was now the breadwinner, Dianne and I were left alone much of the time.

This made my church family all the more important. Our denomination, however, preached and practiced "perfectionism and performance". Since "the great commission" was its central theme, missionaries were at the top of the totem pole. Plus, if you memorize Scripture, know the Bible, attend church every time the doors are open, go on Thursday night visitation - God will bless you and preserve you and your life. No harm can befall you! It was like today's "prosperity theology", only not materialistic, but definitely the path to be a "spiritual giant". Although I was definitely a sinner saved by grace, I was exuberant about serving God and LOVED being in His church with His people, feeling accepted, thus receiving their love. I was at home. Who was I? I was a believer! I loved and trusted God with all my heart and soul.

Having been saved at age 5, when I was age 12 at a summer missionary camp, I committed my life to God to "be a missionary", (partly, in response to the persuasive appeal of the retiring missionary speaker). In case that didn't stick however, I followed up with a "rededication" at age 16 at Lake Swan campground in Florida. I loved these camps and conferences where I sought God's will desperately!

Each summer musical groups from the denomination's several colleges toured churches. That summer, a college male quartet gave a concert at our church in Pensacola. I really was attracted to Bobby Bridges, the cute baritone, but somehow ended up at the after-church party with the pianist, John Stebbins. He was an excellent pianist and I, as a piano student, was mesmerized by his musical talents on the piano and the trumpet.

At the young age of 17, I arrived at Toccoa Falls College as a freshman. After a few months, John Stebbins (a senior) and I were "going steady", his having convinced me that I could be a "missionary" to PA where he planned to be a pastor. I honestly thought that God had led me there, that God had brought us together, that John Stebbins was who he said he was, not the imposter he turned out to be. (I was very naïve. I thought that I "loved him" and he genuinely needed me. After all, love is having your needs met.) He was a minister's son, had grown up in a fishbowl. His dad was pastor of two churches simultaneously, and son, John Jr., was trying to fit into the mold that was set out for him.

But now, who was I? Barely 20 years old, I became a fulltime minister's wife in Pennsylvania. The shock alone of changing cultures from the friendly south to a very legalistic western PA district soon landed me in the proctologist's office. We pastored four different churches over 22 years. With my gift of administration and maybe teaching, and with both of us being musically gifted, we fit together very well as a team. He was a "people person," loving the hobbies of PA where he had grown up – hunting, fishing, golfing. He was a socially acceptable and "performing" individual who had been well trained in the art of "pastoring". Since he used renown theologians' sermons, and had a lifetime of watching his dad perform, plus four years of Bible college to his credit, he did well enough.

When my father-in-law died of cancer in May 1986, my pastor-husband felt freed of his obligation to "Honor thy father and thy mother." He promptly resigned the church, and we separated in June, having nothing in common but two children. He had been counting the days when he could actually "be himself," and not live up to the self-fulfilling prophecy given him. I had discovered years earlier that he had applied to an engineering school after high school graduation, but his parents had hidden the acceptance letter, expecting that he would go to Bible college.

Where did I go? At the age of 42, my life was a shamble, and I had to start over. God was with me when I moved into "the projects" on a hill overlooking Lake Erie. I had asked Him to find me a place to live, and if it had to be the projects, that I get "that apartment on the hill with the big oak tree outside the kitchen window". God answered. So, now, on the bottom of the ash heap with the degenerates, I lived there for two years. I was so depressed and financially broke that I went on welfare and food stamps. While I was very thankful to be "delivered" of an unhappy marriage, my mind and spirit were completely broken. The only bright spot was my children.

John was a freshman at Carnegie Mellon Univ (on Pell grants since I was penniless), and Sherri was a junior at Mercyhurst Prep, a Catholic preparatory high school (paid for with money I had borrowed from my Aunt Lucy). My children and their education were my number one priority. People **asked** me ,"Why did you stay with him so long?" I **shared** with them that I had come from a broken home and didn't want my children to endure the prejudice and hardship that I had, plus I wanted them to be able to be self-supportive, and a good education would guarantee that.

Who was I now? Alone in my bedroom in my small apartment protected by my big oak tree, I definitely was not who I had been because the church denomination in which I had grown up, loved and worked my whole life, didn't know what to do with me. I was a misfit, a displaced person. Pastors in that denomination did NOT divorce. I had to resign as teacher of the young adult S.S. class, after which one member said to me, "No wonder you were such a good teacher, you were living what you taught!" Well, I was suffering greatly and finding refuge in Christ, but I was also totally confused - not knowing what to do. I felt somewhat guilty that I was protecting a liar, so in that respect we were both hypocrites. I had to resign as the Erie County Women's Missionary Prayer Fellowship VP. I was probably an embarrassment to those sweet godly women who prayed very long prayers with lots of Thee's and Thou's. I was deeply wounded, and they didn't know what to do with someone wounded and suffering, who no longer fit the mold of perfectionism and performance. My performance was over. Show canceled.

One night around 11p.m., I was counting my valium tablets and decided before doing anything drastic (as my sister had done previously), I would phone the sweet pastor at the "new denomination" where I had transferred. (After all, our parsonage had received phone calls at all hours 24/7.) The pastor's wife answered the phone, telling me "No, my husband is asleep, and I am not going to awaken him." I thanked her and hung up the phone and said, "Well, God, I guess it's all up to You!" Since psychologically, my husband and I had divorced 10 years earlier after he continually refused to go for counseling, that night I cried out, "Lord, help me, heal me, and isn't there someone on the face of this whole earth who would accept me as I am, that can be a husband to me?"

He led me to Isaiah 43..." Fear not, for I have redeemed thee, I have called thee by thy name; thou art mine. 2 When thou passest through the waters, I will be with thee; and through the rivers, they shall not overflow thee: when thou walkest through the fire, thou shalt not be burned; neither shall the flame kindle upon thee.

3 For I am the LORD thy God, the Holy One of Israel, thy Savior." Then to Isaiah 54:5... "For thy Maker is thine husband; the LORD of hosts is his name; and thy Redeemer the Holy One of Israel; The God of the whole earth shall he be called." "LORD, FORGIVE ME."

By October I got a job at Great Lakes Rehab Hospital as a secretary, so I could now get off welfare. I had become active in that local evangelical church where one Sunday a couple that I did not know approached me and asked if they could give my name and number to a friend of theirs who attended a different church. They said he was a good Christian man, and "We think you two would be ideal for each other!" I was taken aback and replied, "I don't even know you, much less him, so how could you know that?" They said, "We have been watching you..." Strange conversation, but okay Lord....

Almost twenty-five happy years later, while I thank God for His leading and blessings to me, I **ask** myself, and I am still wondering what happened to my earlier life. Where did I go wrong? Wasn't God enough? I honestly thought I was called of God and was in His will. I had followed all the rules. I had made a career of excelling in "suffering, grace, and praise." God, His Word, and precious Holy Spirit were actually all I ever had.

God led Bob and me to North Carolina. For

the first 20 years in NC, I wandered around in a spiritual wilderness, keeping contact with God, but still unsure of my identity, of who I was in Him. Those 20 years, to some people might be considered a loss, but we were Christians going through the motions, but definitely following "at a distance". Bob had grown up in a liberal church and was a fairly new Christian. So, we worked in the church nursery, attending worship and Sunday School whenever it was convenient, but looking back, our jobs definitely came first.

God blessed me with a wonderful administrative job at WFUSM, which fit my talents and personality perfectly. Although I didn't confront anybody spiritually, nor did I have a Bible lying on my desk, I have to believe that my life was a silent witness for God. People knew my background (word gets around). I loved the administrative duties and the respect of my position, assisting in making the department successful and prosperous. God was good. He was healing me, although I rarely opened His Word, nor did I attend any ladies Bible studies. The Department of Anesthesiology was like the family that I'd lost, so I loved and served each faculty and resident happily, as unto the Lord.

Two years before retiring, I had a strong inclination that I should listen to Bob, retire, and join Community Bible Study (he attended an evening class in Charlotte). I was wrong not to listen to Bob's urging back then. I said, "Lord, I trust you, it's Bob I don't trust." Bob had changed jobs several times, and his current position was in limbo since Wells Fargo had recently bought Wachovia. At one point, my mother had **shared** her teacher retirement check with us for 18 months.

Thankfully, God answered prayer! Just before Thanksgiving, 2008, Bob was officially notified that Wells Fargo was going to keep him on, and that very day I submitted my resignation, effective Dec 31. What a relief! I had been as thorough in my secular job as I had been as a pastor's wife. I was tired.

I went to my first CBS meeting in January 2009, thankful that I was welcomed. I loved Ruth and her sweet spirit from day one, when I had driven to her house and picked up my workbook. However, the first month or so at CBS, all I could do was sit and cry through the lectures. While I felt God had brought me "home", I discovered that I was still in much pain. My life and my faith had been shattered. I was angry at God, and I just wasn't so sure I could trust Him again, much less a group of "godly" women. But at my first visit to the leader's group, overhearing Kendall's comment to another leader, tears came to my eyes. She said, "Oh that's Jan, I know her. She's okay."

Who am I? I am forgiven, cleansed, and

restored to fellowship with Christ. He is at work within me. I have **discovered** that He not only has chosen and called me, but He is equipping me; He is renewing, transforming my mind, showing me by His Holy Spirit through His Holy Word, "what is that good, acceptable and perfect will of God." I love and trust God, therefore I will accept whatever He allows in my life, today and in the future. My life is hidden with Christ in God. I am not my own; I am bought with a price. His purpose will be accomplished for His glory; what He has begun, He will complete. His grace is sufficient. Whatever He requires of me, I will trust Him to carry me through. For truly, God is enough.

One of my favorite poems:

'This is from Me,' the Saviour said,
As bending low He kissed my brow.
'For One who loves you thus has led,
Just rest in Me, be patient now.
Your Father knows you have need of this,
Tho', why perchance you cannot see.
Grieve not for things you've seemed to miss,
The thing I send is best for thee.'
Then, looking through my tears, I plead,
'Dear Lord, forgive, I did not know,
Twill not be hard since Thou dost tread
Each path before me here below.
And for my good this thing must be,
His grace sufficient for each test.'
So still I'll sing, 'Whatever be,
God's way for me is always best.'

(Streams in the Desert, 1972)

My favorite song:
He Giveth More Grace

1. He giveth more grace when the burdens grow greater, He sendeth more strength when the labors increase; To added afflictions He added His mercy, to multiplied trials His multiplied peace.

2. When we have exhausted our store of endurance, when our strength has failed ere the day is half done, when we reach the end of our hoarded resources, Our Father's full giving has only begun.

Chorus:
His love has no limits, His grace has no measure, His power has no boundary known unto men,For out of His infinite riches in Jesus He giveth, and giveth, and giveth again.

About - Jan Killmeier

Jeanette (Jan) Browning Jones Killmeier was born Sept 23, 1944, in Anniston, Alabama. She attended Toccoa Falls Academy, GA, then moved to Pensacola, FL in 1960 where she attended Brent Christian School. After high school graduation, she attended Toccoa Falls Bible College (GA) where she received her MRS degree in 1964. From October 1964 to June 1986 (22 yrs.), she and husband pastored four churches (Christian Missionary Alliance). These were located in Pittsburgh, West Middlesex, Brockway, and Union City, PA.

Jan was graduated from Gannon University, Erie, PA in 1986, with an Associate Degree in Business Administration. She worked at Great Lakes Rehab Hospital for two years, then with husband, Bob, moved to Winston-Salem, NC, where she worked as an Administrative Assistant in the Anesthesiology Department of WFUSM from early 1989 to retirement Dec 2008 (20 yrs.). She continues to be active in the church, ladies Bible studies (CBS and BSF), and community volunteerism.

Trust in Him Through All Things
by Doug Shell

It was Nov. 1968, on a plane, headed home from my tour in Vietnam. God had protected me, no doubt in my mind. Now my thoughts turned to what was ahead. What money I had would not last long, so maybe a job until I could decide what I wanted to do. The plane landed in my hometown of Bluefield, WV. As I waited for my duffle bag to be unloaded, on a whim, I **asked** the ticket agent if by chance they were hiring. He said they had just lost an agent to the FAA; would I like an application? I said yes, and filled it out while I waited. The next day I was called in to take the aptitude test on a Friday. I was hired and started to work on Dec 01, 1968, with Piedmont Airlines.

Not long after I got home, I ran into Sharon, who would become my wife. We had gone to school together and rode the same school bus. We knew each other very well, and after a few months dating, we were married. In early 1971, Piedmont built a central reservation center in Winston-Salem, NC. I was low on the seniority list, working rotating shifts and holidays. Sharon and I talked and decided to transfer to Winston-Salem. Because of my experience at the airport, I was put into a department as a go-between with airport agents and reservation agents. We would check with airports on delays or cancellations and put the information in the computer for the reservation agents to pull up for our passengers. It worked very well because it cut down on the phone calls to the airports.

Piedmont builds an Airline Operation Control Center (AOCC) over the hanger at the Winston Salem airport. All the departments that made operation decisions were put into one large room; Dispatch, Maintenance Control, Pilot Scheduling, Flight Attendant Scheduling, and my department, Passenger Movement. These departments had worked together by phone for years, so putting us together was a great idea. It worked so well that other airlines came in to see how it was done.

In 1989, US Air, an airline in the Northeast, bought Piedmont. My job would be moving to Pittsburg, PA. I had to make a choice, to go or stay in Winston-Salem and take another position. I went to Pittsburg to check it out. The cost of living was a lot higher, and also my daughter was a rising senior in high school and did not want to move. After much thought we decided to stay In Winston Salem, and I would take a job in schedule change. This was mainly proofing the flight schedules to make sure they lined up with connecting flights. This lasted about five years.

One day I was **asked** if I would be interested in

working in cargo sales. There would be four of us working only by telephone to boost sales. I said I would, and we were given 800 numbers so our clients could call us for special rates or problems they might be having. This worked extremely well. Now there was a special department of 30 agents, set up in Washington D.C. This only lasted a few years for me.

I then went into a department that worked flight cancellations and delays by calling passengers. I would load the passenger list from a flight, and we had 35 agents that would call and rebook our passengers on another flight. While I was in this department, we went on a four-day all-inclusive trip to Mexico. It was a special for airline agents. On the day we were to leave to fly back home, 911 happened. We were stranded for eight extra days. The Mexican Government payed for our hotel room and we paid for our meals. It was a very stressful time, not knowing what was going on, and the communication to the U. S. was terrible. The hotel gave everyone the Conference Room one day, and people filled it up to pray. After eight long days we were able to fly back home.

My stress level was high by this time, and I thought I was handling it well. Not long after returning to work, I learned of a new department that was being created. It would be a department to oversee all the reservation offices. I decided to apply. I went through two interviews and was one of eight chosen. Our job was to keep track of calls in and out of each reservation office. I was three years into this job and started to **discover** rumors of another merger. My co-workers were talking about it every day. The stress level was climbing each day. I had made all the decisions on my own along the way, but I realized it was just too much to handle alone. There was so much unknown that we had to watch our spending of large sums of money, like buying a car or things like that. The stress was weighing me down. It was like a big black cloud hanging over my head. Then one day my co-workers **were sharing, big time,** on what was going to happen. Were we going to lose our jobs, or be transferred or even move to another city? All sorts of things were brought up and talked about. Then, in a couple of days came the word. Our department would be moving to Phoenix, AZ. Boy, did that ever get the talk started!

That was it for me; I turned it all over to the Lord in prayer. I prayed for His guidance and I **asked** Him to take away the pressure I was under. The Lord is faithful; it was right away that the pressure was gone, the black cloud was gone, and I had a peace that I hadn't had in a long time. My co-workers noticed it right away. They would **ask** "Aren't you worried?" I would smile and say, "No, I turned it over to the Lord and He will handle it. I will be good with whatever happens."

When they would share about it in the following days, I would just grin and go on with my work. Then the Lord answered prayer. As the merger drew near, the top boss that wanted us to move to Phoenix, got replaced. The new boss came to our office to **discover** firsthand what we did. We had a room full of computers and hardware equipment that would let us reroute calls from one reservation center to another in case of power loss or some type of emergency. After the tour he said it would cost too much to move all this equipment to Phoenix. "You can keep doing your work right here in Winston-Salem." The Lord is good! Not only did we stay in Winston, we got a much bigger role in the operation. I was able to retire at the end of 2014!

Looking back over my life I can see how the Lord has always been there for me. As I was growing up, I got involved in sports. I know now that it kept me out of trouble. In Vietnam the Lord was with me every step of the way. When I returned home, he led Sharon to that service station for us to meet up again. He was there at the airport when I applied for the job. He was there when I was changing departments. He has been with me since I asked Jesus into my heart as a seventeen year-old. It's easy to take things for granted when things are going good in your life. I was guilty of calling on the Lord just in bad times. **Now I've discovered** and learned to thank

Him for the good things too, especially my 46-year Airline Career.

About - Douglas (Doug) Shell

I grew up in the southern mountains of West Virginia. Got started in sports at an early age. Played football, basketball, and ran track all through school. Was drafted into the army in 1966 and did a tour in Vietnam. Started my airline career in 1968 that lasted 46 years with a move to Winston-Salem, NC. Joined Calvary Baptist Church in 1971, and still a member today. I live in Davie County now.

I'm a member of the Clemmons VFW Post 1910, and also a member of the Honor Guard.

Enjoying retirement with my wife, Sharon, and my two kids, along with 7 grandchildren and 2 great grandchildren.

God Shows up in the Midst of Trials
by Joe Boone

When we moved into our house in 1974, we experienced some trials in our life. We visited Calvary and counseled with the pastor, Dr. Corts. We started attending Calvary, and God began working in our life.

In 1971, I went to work for Westinghouse Electric Corporation in Rural Hall, NC. I worked for Westinghouse in the Quality Control Department as a Quality Assurance Technician. When Siemens bought Westinghouse after 31 years, I transferred to Charlotte, NC to work at that Siemens plant.

Then in 1974, I began a great adventure that God had in store for me. John 10:10 (Christ speaking) - "I came that they might have life and have it more abundantly, that it might be full and meaningful.", and 2 Corinthians 5:17 – "Therefore, if any man be in Christ, he is a new creation, old things are passed away; behold all things are become new." God fulfilled these two promises in my life when I **asked** Jesus into my life.

I grew up in a Methodist church, and I had never heard a gospel presentation. A supervisor was **sharing** his testimony at work with an employee, and I overheard his presentation.

After he finished **sharing**, I asked him how I could know that I was saved. He told me if I confessed my sins and received Christ by faith, I would be saved. He **shared** the death, burial and resurrection of Jesus with me. By faith, I received Christ.

My wife and I had been visiting Calvary Church, and shortly thereafter, joined the church. We went through the new member's class, which was customary for new members.

One day Dr. Corts took me into his office and **asked** me about when I was saved. At the time, I was so spiritually immature that I did not know how to express or describe the spiritual transformation that had occurred in my life. That is when Dr. Corts **shared** with me how I could **learn to share my faith** and testimony through his evangelism "share life" program.

We went through his evangelism class as a trainee and **discovered** how to train others.

Listed below are Dr. Corts' steps for **sharing** the Gospel:
1. Look for common interest so you can build a rapport with them.
2. Bridge over to their religious background to see where they are at spiritually.
3. **Ask** qualifying questions to **discover** if they are a Christian. If they do not qualify as a Christian, **ask** them if you can **share**

what the Bible teaches about God's love, man's sin, and sin's penalty.

4. If yes, we would use scripture from the Bible or the Four Spiritual Laws.
   - a. God's Love
   - b. Man's Sin
   - c. Jesus – God's only provision
   - d. Receiving Christ

5. **Ask** if they would like to pray and receive Christ into their heart.

6. If they did pray, I would **share** these scriptures for assurance:
   - a. Christ came into your life. (Revelation 3:20)
   - b. Your sins were forgiven. (Colossians 1:14)
   - c. You became a child of God. (John 1:12)
   - d. You received eternal life. (John 5:24)
   - e. You began the great adventure for which God created you. (John 10:10)

Example of sharing the Gospel through friendship evangelism:

At work, God gave me an opportunity to **share** with three different people and to train them using the "share life" program, and later, many more members at Calvary.

One Sunday, my wife and I visited Center Grove Baptist Church, and the pastor **shared** with the congregation about one prayer God would alway answer. It is that if we pray for an opportunity to **share** our faith and testimony, He is faithful and will provide.

That week God answered my prayer. While in Charlotte, my friend and I had the opportunity to **share** our testimony and the Gospel with a salesman. My friend gave his testimony, and I **shared** the gospel with this salesman about the death, burial, and resurrection of Jesus Christ, and because of that **discovery**, he prayed to receive Christ.

God has given me many opportunities to **share** my faith because I took Dr. Corts' evangelism class. If your heart is open and are willing to **share**, the opportunity is there. Proverbs 11:30 - "The fruit of the righteous is a tree of life; and he that winneth souls is wise." **Discover** how you can change a person's life.

About - Joe Boone

I worked at Westinghouse and Siemens Corporation for a total of 36 years before retiring, but I still find opportunities to share my faith. After we became members of Calvary, we became involved in evangelism, teaching the youth for several years. I am now involved in the Gideon ministry.

My wife worked for Calvary for about a year. She stayed at home until our children started school. She worked for Western Electric, US Airways, and Wake Forest Baptist Hospital. While working for the airlines, we had many opportunities to travel.

Dad, I Want to be Like You.
by Tom Dickens

This is a story that I have told many times. I enjoy **sharing** it because it involves a family member. His name is Ray, and he is my nephew.

Ray, as a teenager, got heavily into the drug culture in a big way. He was a heartache for his parents. He would leave home and be gone for weeks at a time. Most times when his family heard from him, he was calling from jail.

Ray's dad spent several years in army aviation, both in active duty, and then several more years with the North Carolina Army National Guard aviation unit. Ray's dad had a heart attack while still on duty and retired as a Lt. Colonel. Without giving specific dates, Ray met with his dad at home, and his dad **shared** this with his son; "Son, your mother and I have given you all the advice that we know to give you, and it does not seem to do any good." He also **shared**, "If this is the road that you want to continue to take, we will not interfere with your plans anymore." Ray said to his dad, **"Dad, I want to be like you."** His dad said, "What do you mean, "Be like me?" He then said, "Son, the army does not take criminals."

Ray **discovered** he needed to act, then wrote a testimony regarding his past involvement with drugs. His letter basically said, "I have been a heartache to my parents, I have been a disgrace to lots of people. I have been running from God. I know if change is to happen, I must do the changing, and I am ready to start now. I need a second chance to prove that I can and will change." Ray **shared** with his father that he wanted to go to flight school and become an aviator like him.

His father took the letter to General Davis, who was in charge of the Army Aviation Unit, showed him the letter, and **asked**, "General, can my son get in the army with a criminal record?" The general said, "Not at my pay grade. This decision would have to be made at the Pentagon level. And, by the way, I am going to the Pentagon tomorrow, and I will be sure that the right person sees the letter."

About 1:00 PM the next day, the general called Ray's dad and said, "Your son is going in the Army!!!!" Ray accomplished his goal, and on September 10, 2001, he was promoted to Lt. Colonel.

By this time, he was on staff at the Pentagon, and I heard that a hi-jacked plane had crashed into the Pentagon. The next day I called his mother and asked if she had heard from Ray. I was concerned that he may have been hurt or killed. She said that he woke up on September 11, 2001 with "the sniffles" and decided to stay at home. I **asked** his mom, "Where did he sit in relation to where the plane hit the Pentagon?"

She said that if he had been at his desk that day, the plane would have "Got him!"

Where there is a will, there is a way. I hope this story will be helpful to anyone struggling with drugs.

About - Tom Dickens

Tom is married to Carolyn Dickens, and they have six children and 15 grandchildren. Professionally, for over 38-year, Tom continues to be an investment agent with Primerica. Prior to that, Tom worked in Israel as a part of the Camp David Peace Treaty (Camp David Accords) building airports.

A Tragic Accident Becomes a Gateway
by Kathy McGuire Tharp

March 31, 1956 was a life-changing day for me and my family. I was a bouncy, blonde, curly headed six year old – always curious, often precocious and considered life my own personal adventure. Very early in the morning, while my mom was tending my newborn sister, she sent me on a little errand downstairs. Our beautiful living room was "off limits" unless I was wearing my party shoes. That sparkling spring morning, the sunshine was streaming in and I couldn't resist tiptoeing in and sitting on the love seat. On the coffee table was an ornate silver cigarette lighter I had seen used on many occasions. It was pretty, fascinating, and I couldn't resist picking it up and playing with it, pretending to be a big girl.

In an instant, when I flicked the lighter, it fell and caught my flannel nightgown on fire. My first thought was that I would be in so much trouble for going into the living room, because I knew I wasn't supposed to be in there. I had never heard of "tuck and roll", so I ran to the nearest faucet to extinguish the flames. I was too little to reach, so with my nightgown in flames, I ran up the stairs screaming. My mom came running out of the baby's room and wrapped her arms around me to pat out the flames. She burned her hands and arms in the process, and realizing she couldn't contain the flames, she firmly placed her hand beneath my chin to protect my face from the fire. She whisked me into her shower to finally extinguish the flames that had threatened to claim her firstborn little girl.

My blonde curls were singed and matted; my burned nightgown draped my little body with shreds of black char, stuck to what was left of my skin. Of course, in shock, I can remember telling my mom I was fine and didn't need to go to the hospital. Dad was out of town and Mom couldn't dial a phone because she had severely burned her hands and arms in her efforts to save me. Through an open window, she was able to awaken a neighbor for help. Gratefully, she called my grandmother and our pediatrician, who was a family friend. With me wrapped in a crisp, white sheet, we were all whisked away in our doctor's private car to St. Louis Children's Hospital, because he knew that was the best place for me to have a chance at survival. Gratefully, our dear neighbor was there to care for my baby sister.

At the hospital, my grandmother stayed with me, while Mom was taken to adjoining Barnes Hospital to care for her burns. As you can imagine, this whole experience set off an unforgettable chain of events, the first hurdle of which was keeping me alive. We were supported by countless prayers from near and far, our precious family and friends that wouldn't let me go, and most of all, our great God who wanted me to not just survive, but to thrive. We were blessed with a world class medical team of doctors, plastic surgeons and nurses who became became lifelong friends. Miraculously, we all celebrated the victory when my 6 month long hospital stay was over.

ASKING

Of course, all of this would cause any number of us to be ASKING "Why?" "Why were so many people praying for me?" "Why would I be scarred for the rest of my life from a childhood accident with 2nd and 3rd degree burns over 70% of my body?" "Why would I undergo countless, excruciatingly painful dressing changes?" "Why would I have to learn to walk again?" "Why would I have more than 30 skin grafts over the next 7 years?" "Why would I be stared at, talked about, not chosen for sports teams, have what seemed like never-ending nightmares?" For me, ASKING the more important question became, "How will I respond to all to these situations?"

DISCOVERING

I DISCOVERED the power of prayer. Had I not felt loved before, I surely DISCOVERED the length and breadth of my family's love for me. My mother, grandmother and I formed an incredible bond in that 6 month hospital stay and beyond... a bond I've DISCOVERED could survive anything, even death. I DISCOVERED the cure for not letting my scars determine who I am or can become. My mom taught me the difference between my body and my soul. My body has scars, but my soul is beautiful, indwelled by the Holy Spirit ~ my countenance shines because of Him. I DISCOVERED inner strength and courage to tolerate pain that I really didn't understand, but would need later in other difficult times. I DISCOVERED compassionate hearts in strangers as well as people who barely knew me and then became friends. I DISCOVERED the world didn't revolve around me and that others might benefit from my plight. My dad was a pilot for Monsanto Chemical Company and a dear friend of the founder, Edgar M. Queeny. He knew me and was so moved by my tragedy that he enlisted all his resources to create a chemical used in flame retardant sleepwear for children. Of course, in 50+ years those DISCOVERIES have been eclipsed by others, but awareness was heightened way back then, undoubtedly saving many children's lives. I DISCOVERED that even in pain and disability, joy wins the day. In fact, I want my epitaph to be "Joyful and Triumphant!"

SHARING

I learned about SHARING - if you look people in the eye and explain something they see as fearful or unfamiliar, they are usually calmed, and camaraderie can emerge. SHARING your tragedies as well as your triumphs has a miraculous, confidence-building effect on others. SHARING involves vulnerability, and when you "get real" with someone in a similar situation, it can break chains that have bound them for years, giving them courage to grow. SHARING your smile and zest for life can be contagious, especially when the chips are down. A "poor me" attitude has never worked for anyone, so let me SHARE with you how valuable it is, in spite of your circumstances, to choose joy.

ASKING, DISCOVERING and SHARING are glorious gateways to growing in Christ. As we journey through this life on our way to eternity, we must ASK hard questions, DISCOVER truths that become our sure foundation, and SHARE with others to lighten their load and enhance their journey along the way.

"Every morning, lean your arms upon the windowsill of heaven and gaze upon the Lord; and with that vision in your heart, turn strong to meet the day." Thomas Blake

About - Kathy McGuire Tharp

Kathy was born in St. Louis, MO in 1949, with a smile that has rarely left her face! Even in Kindergarten, her teachers were overjoyed as well as challenged by Kathy's zest for life. Her vibrant spirit remained through the horrors of her accident in 1956. With great encouragement from her family and countless prayers of many, a course of joy and gratitude was set for Kathy's life. She attended the University of Kentucky, and although her studies were somewhat engaging, she ultimately embarked on a career in Real Estate that spanned over three decades. During an interview for a Real Estate Sales Secretary position, Kathy met John McGuire. Kathy always had a twinge of uneasiness with new people, because she wasn't sure she would be accepted because of her scars. After the interview, she asked John if her scars bothered him. John looked up from his desk and smiled. Without a word, he took her scarred hand in his, kissed it, and then went right back to work. Kathy got the job... acceptance is a wonderful thing.

Two and a half years later, Kathy and John were married. With contagious enthusiasm, they served many families' Real Estate needs, helping them achieve their dreams. All the awards were appreciated, but the greatest rewards were the trust, confidence, and camaraderie with their clients that lasted far beyond any Real Estate transaction. John and Kathy shared a deep devotion for their Lord and

Savior, Jesus Christ. His presence in their lives made all the difference in the way they approached the gift of life to share with others for over 32 years.

When John passed away in 2009, Kathy decided to retire from active service in Real Estate. During this time of deep grief, Kathy began to attend GriefShare, a Christian grief support ministry, which was a lifesaver for her. As she was healing from the loss of John, she could feel the Lord's presence more and more, encouraging her to reach out to others who were hurting. Kathy became a facilitator for GriefShare, helping others discover a new, abundant life beyond their loss.

Kathy was also was able to reengage in encouraging other burn survivors to see the gift of life waiting beyond their immediate crisis. One family's story is unforgettable. Beautiful, twin teenage girls and their family had their lives changed forever when one of them suffered horrible, disfiguring burns in a tragic car crash. Kathy counseled their parents and met their daughter in the burn unit. One day, Kathy asked her, "What are your dreams?" She said she wanted to go to Africa and teach English to children. They discussed many aspects of what would be required of her to accomplish that. Kathy clearly remembers how this young girl, in excruciating pain, would miraculously light up and even become animated at the prospect of actually achieving her dream. When she went home from the hospital, Kathy lost touch with this sweet family, but often wondered what happened to this dear young girl. Years later, Kathy was in the grocery store when a woman came up to her and asked, "Aren't you Kathy?" She said yes, and she asked if Kathy remembered counseling her family in the burn unit. Kathy said, "Of course, I remember you, and how is your daughter doing?" She smiled and with tears in her eyes, told Kathy they had just put their daughter on a plane to Africa. Their embrace was long and so sweet. Kathy will never forget this grateful mother whispering, "Thank you."

In 2012, Kathy met Michael Tharp, who had also lost his wife of many years to cancer. As their friendship grew, Kathy felt that familiar uneasiness about her scars, so she asked Mike if they were a turn off to him. With unflinching honesty, he smiled and said, "No. I see them as your decorations of courage." Mike and Kathy also saw in each other the love of Christ. He revealed a surprising, life-changing path before them, and they were married in 2013. Mike had also attended GriefShare after the loss of his wife, and benefited by it greatly. In one of their first endeavors as a married couple, Mike and Kathy began serving in GriefShare together. They find it so rewarding to see dear ones enveloped in grief begin to open like the petals of a flower, taking in the light of God's Word, then finding their new place and purpose in life again. Mike and Kathy also share a love for Bible study, photography, travel, exploring natural beauty, and riding their Can Am on woodsy two lane back roads. In 2015, they were rescued by Milo, their loveable Golden Boxer, and he loves to tag along on their adventures.

Although Kathy lost her precious grandmother in 1989, her deep love, humor and guiding light will always be in Kathy's heart. Her beloved mom passed away in 2019, and as you can imagine with all they shared, the loss of her was especially difficult for Kathy. Gratefully, she inherited her mom's effervescent joy, love of surprises, and an indescribable bond of love that will be with her forever. Kathy's mom's life verse was Psalm 118:24. "This is the day the Lord has made; let us rejoice and be glad in it!" And that she did, to the benefit of all who knew her. GriefShare has once again played a major role in Kathy's healing, because she knows only too well that the love of Christ will see her through. Kathy will always carry with her the love and encouragement lavished on her by these two exceptional women because they would stop at nothing to assure Kathy that she was meant to shine. By the Grace of God, the indwelling of the Holy Spirit has made that a reality.

CHAPTER SIX

Putting it All Together

I was struggling, trying to put my thoughts together for this final chapter, when on a Monday morning, September 7th at 6:20 AM, I heard four very loud knocks on our front door. I got up out of bed, slipped downstairs, and looked out the window of the front door. I saw no one, so I walked over to look out on our deck at the driveway, and saw no car, no person, nothing. I moved to the kitchen, peered out the front window, and saw no one. I finally tiptoed back upstairs, finding Susan still asleep, and I crawled back into bed. Then it was as Someone said, "Now that I have your attention, this is what you should say in the final chapter." My wife never heard the knocking on the door; only me! When she awoke, I shared this with her and mentioned that I now understood what should be said in this final chapter.

Have you ever stopped and looked back on your life at the things that you tried to put together? Growing up as a child, there are many things that I put together, and I have vivid memories of all the plastic models that I built; models of boats, planes, cars, and people. If you recall doing this yourself, whenever you tried to put those things together, there was always a set of instructions. Do we always follow the instructions? For me, the thrill was opening the box, looking at all the parts, and trying to imagine what connects with what, without even looking at the instructions. For some models, it was easy to observe and determine what went where. Some models were more complex, yet all the parts were there, and I knew there would be a final assembly. However, with the complexity, instructions definitely needed to be followed for the results that would be desired.

There are also things that I took apart, not to be destructive, but that would be instructive. I guess we could call it reverse engineering. Sometimes we have to break things down to see how things really work, see what parts function where and why, and what parts need the most attention. While this chapter is about putting things together, let us be reminded that we have to be introspective and take things apart so we can discover the true workings, at times. This applies to our family, our work, and our faith.

I'm sure you have heard the expression that we need to have a balance in our life. Well, life is a balancing act, and that is certainly true. I am sure that in our lives, each of us have, at some point, lost our balance. We have gotten out of balance, and we have fallen, and it is hard! Sometimes the fall could have caused injury, emotionally and/or physically, but we then try to regain balance in our life.

If you are out of balance now, and want to regain that balance, what is the most important thing that you can do in your life at this moment? To regain that balance, it must first begin with you, and it has to be internal, starting with your heart and your faith. Your heart-life must not only be strong but put together correctly. If not, then you will continue to be out of balance, and on an undetermined pathway in your life, that affects the life of others who are connected to you. The first rebuilding must take place in your heart.

> Proverbs 4 v23 "Above all else, guard your heart, for everything you do flows from it."

> Romans 12 v2 "And be not conformed to this world, but be ye transformed by the renewing of your mind, that ye may prove what is the good, and acceptable, and perfect will of God."

Now might just be the perfect time in your life to start **asking**, **discovering**, and **sharing**. Now might just be the perfect time in your life to pick yourself up, dust yourself off, and continue with a new energy and enthusiasm. Now might just be the time in your life not to be a follower but to be a leader. Now might just be the time in your life to see truth instead of believing everything others have to say without substantiating the facts. Now just might be the time that your life will have a significant impact on others. Now might be the time to start putting it all together.

Step 1: Putting Faith in your Heart

Begin first with your faith, second with love. This will be the key to the treasure chest of **asking**, **discovering**, and **sharing** as illustrated below.

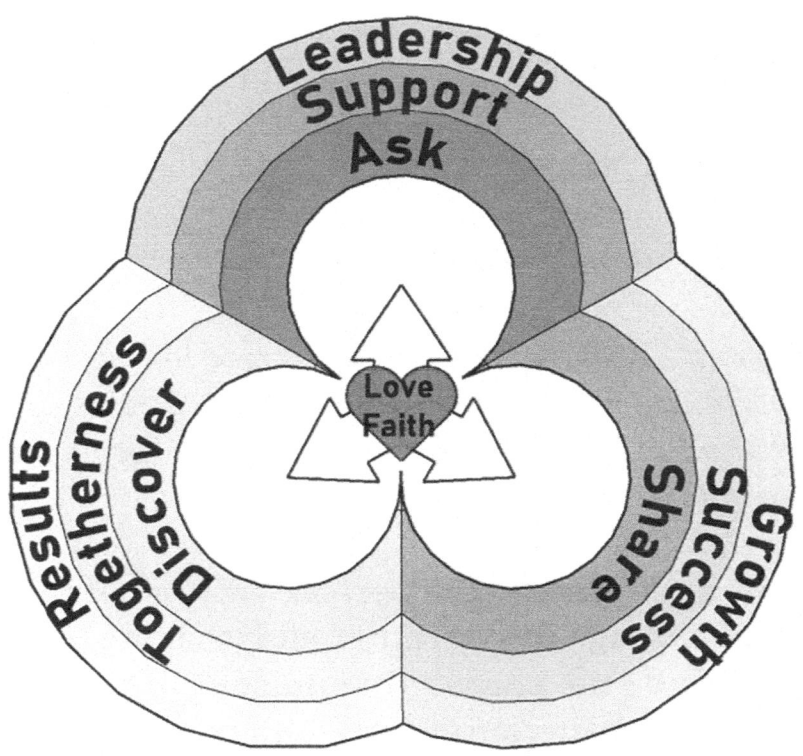

- Be willing to perform open heart surgery on yourself; not physical but spiritual.

- Be willing to open your heart by reconnecting with your faith. Sometimes we believe something so strongly in our heart, it is hard for us to change, even when we know something is not the truth.

- Be willing to ask questions about faith and your faith. Not until then, will you be able to discover the balance return in your life because you are finally putting it all together. But now, most importantly, you will be able to share that balance and discovery with others.

- Be willing to strengthen your heart. To do that you must connect or reconnect with these scriptures. Here are some of my favorites:

Mark 12 v30 "And you shall love the Lord your God with all your heart and with all your soul and with all your mind and with all your strength."

Psalm 46 v1 "My flesh and my heart may fail, but God is the strength of my heart and my portion forever."

• Be willing to talk to God and listen. What better source to ask, discover and share with, than to be in prayer with your Creator?

Step 2: Love

Love and faith are connected, you can have one without the other, but that would make you incomplete, and who wants to be an incomplete person? Use these love steps to help you be completed in love.

• Be willing to love God with all your heart and soul.

Matthew 22:37
"Jesus replied, 'Love the Lord your God with all your heart and with all your soul and with all your mind."

• Be willing to love sincerely.

Romans 12 v9
"Love must be sincere. Hate what is evil; cling to what is good."

• Be willing to take your love into the workplace for the success of others.

1 Corinthians 10 v24
"No one should seek their own good, but the

good of others."

- Be willing to become an example of love to others, as you don't know the impact you have made on them.

Hebrews 13 v1-2
"Keep on loving one another as brothers and sisters. Do not forget to show hospitality to strangers, for by so doing some people have shown hospitality to angels without knowing it."

- Be willing, in love, to forgive and to ask for forgiveness. Do not hesitate to ask for forgiveness.

Psalm 86 v5
"You, Lord, are forgiving and good, abounding in love to all who call to you."

So, as you finish this book, the two most important steps are those of Faith and Love. But you must be willing, and I repeat, you must be willing, to set your faith and love correctly, as indicated in the previous two steps. When those steps are set correctly, and you begin **asking**, **discovering**, and **sharing**, it will lead you to togetherness, successes, growth, and leadership; then the results will be the fulfillment of God's plans for you.

So, remember this:

Never Stop!
Asking
Discovering
Sharing

Make a change in your life and others!

About the Author

Mr. Burns received a B. of Arch. from the University of Kentucky, and a Master of Science in Interior Design from UNCG. Herb has over 39 years' experience in higher education. at Forsyth Technical Community College. He has received numerous awards for excellence in teaching and leadership in education and technology. As an educator, he has created and taught over a dozen new courses relating to architecture, animation and digital design, and is recognized as an pioneer and innovator in this field. He is a licensed architect. His knowledge and skills are also known internationally as a guest lecturer on digital design, architecture, sustainability, and best business practices in Finland, Belarus, Russia, and Ukraine. Mr. Burns was also a Fulbright Scholar. He is a founding collaborator of the Center for Design Innovation, Piedmont Triad Design Consortium, founding collaborator of Design Leadershop, and past president of ABRO Winston-Salem.

Mr. Burns has served as Interim Dean of Engineering at Forsyth Technical Community College, also as the Department Chair for Design Technologies, including programs of study in Architecture, Interior Design, Radio & Television, and Digital Effects & Animation. He was the Program

Coordinator for the DEA Program, and he served as the Coordinator of International Partnerships at Forsyth Technical Community College.

Mr. Burns is the president of HB Studios, which includes services for architectural and interior design, digital content, publishing, international, business and education consulting. https://hibssb.myportfolio.com Mr. Burns is a host on the popular podcast series, "Three Men for Thee" https://3-mft.fireside.fm, and is also the author of a best-selling book: "Route 66 – Have You Found Your Route in Life?"; an illustrated journey through each book of the Bible, with historical content and applications for today's Christian living. All illustrations were created by the author.

ROU†E 66

HAVE YOU FOUND YOUR
ROUTE IN LIFE?

HERBERT I. BURNS JR.

This book can be purchased at:
https://store.bookbaby.com/book/Route-66
To schedule a speaking engagement email:
HerbBurns@mail.com

Acknowledgements

This is a very special section of this book for me, as I want to acknowledge my family, friends, and mentors who have inspired me, led me, encouraged me, rebuked me, loved me, mentored me, trusted me, and taught me. I must start with my family; my mother, Anna Burns; her parents, Sphar and Patti Bruner, where I lived with my mother. Also, the entire Burklow family; my Aunt Lillian, Uncle Duke, and their children; Sphar, Nancy, Raymond, Becky, Duke Jr, and Harold. They all are especially important in my upbringing. Today, I still think of Becky as my sister.

Outside of family, there are those that have influenced me in ways that they may never know. Don and Mary Haley Hancock. Don was my high school basketball coach. Also, Sara Tate, and Vito Girone, my architecture professors. I also want to thank Forsyth Technical Community College, which was my first job after graduation from college. There I was able to **ask**, **discover**, and **share** with my students, colleagues, and administrators. There I was able to vision for the future and apply my ideas, and dreams. For almost forty years at the college, I was blessed to be gifted by God; to enlighten, educate, enrich, engage, and empower students to be their best and to be a leader in their journey.

A special thanks to my wife, Susan, who is my incredible supporter and encourager. Susan also edits my writing. "The end results of what I write is much better because of you. Thank you, Honey!"

When writing, it's also important to get views from others. Special thanks go out to John Valley, John Moormann, Clif Arnold, and Bob Hicks for their thoughtful reviews, which are on the back cover of the book.

Incredibly unique to this book is Chapter Five, "Experiences of Others". This chapter contains amazing stories in the lives of others, and how **asking**, **discovering**, and **sharing** have been transformative in their life. I give thanks again to these special people: Gary Griffith, Henry Williamson, Charles Morrison, Jack Bales, Slavik Pyzh, J.C. Martin, Steve Whitley, Linwood Lewis, Kenny Patrick, Jerry Pegram, Jan Killmeier, Doug Shell, Joe Boone, Tom Dickens, and Kathy McGuire Tharp.

Bonus

This might be the first time that you have ever seen something like this in a book. As an author/educator, I want to acknowledge and recognize your success in reading this unique book, with a certificate of achievement.

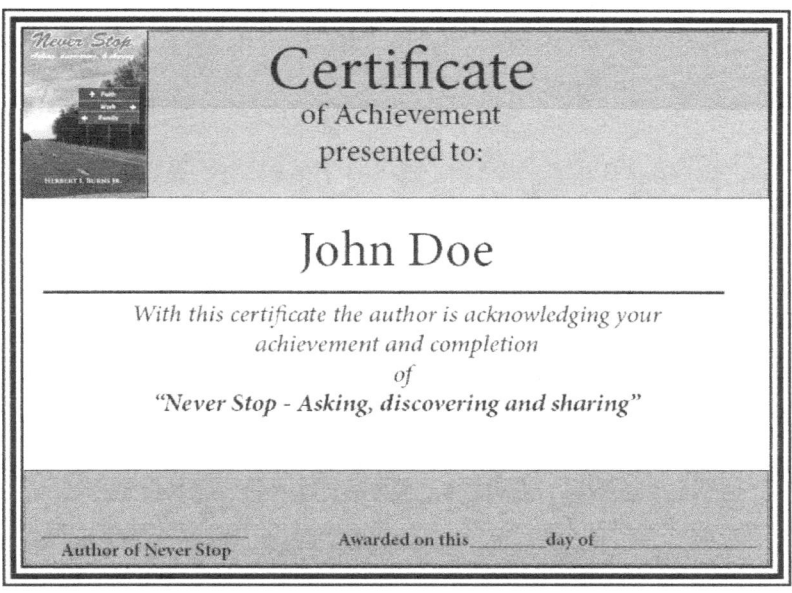

To receive this signed certificate from the author, send the following information to:

HerbBurns@mail.com

1. A photograph of you with the book
2. A short review of the book

Upon receiving this information, the author will send you a signed certificate of achievement.